MUSIC IN THE THEATER

PRINCETON STUDIES IN OPERA

CAROLYN ABBATE AND ROGER PARKER,
SERIES EDITORS

Reading Opera, edited by Arthur Groos and
Roger Parker (1988)

Puccini's "Turandot": The End of the Great Tradition
by William Ashbrook and Harold Powers (1991)

*Unsung Voices: Opera and Musical Narrative in the
Nineteenth Century* by Carolyn Abbate (1991)

Wagner Androgyne: A Study in Interpretation
by Jean-Jacques Nattiez,
translated by Stewart Spencer (1993)

*Music in the Theater: Essays on Verdi and
Other Composers* by Pierluigi Petrobelli,
with translations by Roger Parker (1994)

MUSIC IN THE THEATER

ESSAYS ON VERDI AND OTHER COMPOSERS

Pierluigi Petrobelli

WITH
TRANSLATIONS
BY
Roger Parker

PRINCETON UNIVERSITY
PRESS

Published by Princeton University Press, 41 William Street,
Princeton, New Jersey 08540
In the United Kingdom: Princeton University Press,
Chichester, West Sussex

Library of Congress Cataloging-in-Publication Data

Petrobelli, Pierluigi.
Music in the theater : essays on Verdi and other composers /
Pierluigi Petrobelli ; translated by Roger Parker.
p. cm. — (Princeton studies in opera)
Translated from Italian.
Includes bibliographical references.
ISBN 0-691-09134-X
1. Verdi, Giuseppe, 1813–1901. 2. Opera. I. Series.
ML410.V4P28 1994
782.1—dc20 93-3440

This book has been composed by Meg Freer in Monotype Bembo,
using Bestinfo's PageWright composition software
Designed by Jan Lilly
Music typeset by Don Giller

Princeton University Press books are printed on
acid-free paper, and meet the guidelines for permanence
and durability of the Committee on
Production Guidelines for Book Longevity of
the Council on Library Resources

Printed in the United States of America

2 4 6 8 10 9 7 5 3 1

CONTENTS

ACKNOWLEDGMENTS

A NUMBER OF these chapters first appeared in Italian and are published here in English for the first time: chapter 1 first appeared as "Nabucco," in *Conferenze 1966–1967* (Associazione amici della Scala) (Milan, n.d.), 15–47; chapter 2 as "Verdi e il *Don Giovanni*. Osservazioni sulla scena iniziale del *Rigoletto*," in *Atti del primo congresso internazionale di studi verdiani* (Parma, 1969), 232–46; chapter 3 as "Osservazioni sul processo compositivo in Verdi," in *Acta musicologica* 43 (1971), 125–43; chapter 4 as "Pensieri per *Alzira*," in *Nuove prospettive nella ricerca verdiana* (Atti del convegno internazionale in occasione della prima del "Rigoletto" in edizione critica) (Parma, 1987), 110–24; chapter 9 as "La concezione drammatico-musicale dell'*Alceste* (Milan, 1767)," in *Gluck in Wien*, ed. Gerhard Croll and Monika Woitas (vol. 1 of *Gluck-Studien*) (Kassel, 1987), 131–38; chapter 10 as "Note sulla poetica di Bellini. A proposito de *I puritani*," in *Muzikoloski Zbornik*, vol. 8 (Ljubljana, 1972), 70–84; and chapter 11 as "Bellini e Paisiello. Altri documenti sulla nascita dei *Puritani*," in *Il melodramma italiano dell'Ottocento. Studi e ricerche per Massimo Mila* (Turin, 1977), 351–63. Chapter 5 first appeared as "Per un'esegesi della struttura drammatica del *Trovatore*," in *Atti del III° congresso internazionale di studi verdiani* (Parma, 1974), 387–400; the present English translation (by William Drabkin), lightly edited here, appeared in *Music Analysis* 1 (1982): 129–41. Chapter 6 first appeared in English, in James Redmond, ed., *Drama, Dance, and Music* (Themes in Drama, no. 3) (Cambridge, 1981), 129–42. The introduction and chapters 7 and 8 are new to this volume.

THE REALIZATION of this book would have been impossible without the help of colleagues, students, and friends who contributed over the years to the clarification of the ideas that form its gist. I remember particularly the reports—and ensuing discussion—of the students of my first Verdi seminar, at the Graduate Center of the City University of New York during the fall semester 1970; and those of the participants in the seminar on the same subject in the Faculty of Music, University of London, King's College, in 1974. Julian Budden and Frits Noske have been playing—with patience as well as interest—time and again the role of touchstone for many hypotheses and assertions, placing at my disposal their deep knowledge of the repertory as well as their own hypotheses and conclusions—a particularly rewarding and satisfying intellectual exercise. Walter Lippincott was extremely receptive from the beginning to the proposal of bringing the project under his editorial wing; Elizabeth Powers, also of Princeton University Press, has constantly offered in a most graceful manner her editorial—as well as diplomatic—talents; and I am very much indebted to Lauren Oppenheim, who skillfully and patiently edited this volume. Finally, I would like to express my very special debt of gratitude to Roger Parker. It was his idea in the first place to publish in the form of a book the essays I had written about musical theater; he introduced me to the publisher and included my text in the series overseen by him and Carolyn Abbate; and he took upon himself the tiresome and demanding task of translating into readable English my idiomatic and often idiosyncratic Italian prose and, especially, stimulated a particularly dispersive author to bring to an end the task to which he had committed himself—that of completing the book. It seems particularly appropriate, then, to dedicate this volume to him, as well as to Lynden, Matthew, Emma, and Tom, with gratitude and affection.

Pierluigi Petrobelli

Rome, 8 September 1992

A NOTE ON ITALIAN PROSODY

FREQUENT reference is made in this book to the metrical structure of Italian poetry. It seems advisable to summarize briefly for the English-speaking reader some of its basic features, especially those mentioned more often.

An Italian poetic line is measured by, and named after, its number of syllables and the position of its final accent. The syllable-count designations are as follows: *quinario* (five syllables), *senario* (six syllables), *settenario* (seven syllables), *ottonario* (eight syllables), *novenario* (nine syllables; very rare in nineteenth-century prosody), *decasillabo* (ten syllables), and *endecasillabo* (eleven syllables). A line is called *tronco* (truncated) when the accent falls on the last syllable of the final word: andrò, pietà, amor. It is *piano* (plain)—by far the most frequent category—when the accent falls on the penultimate syllable of the final word: pensièro, fidùcia, beàto. It is *sdrucciolo* (slippery) when the accent falls on the antepenultimate syllable of the final word: sòrgono, intrèpido.

The standard for measuring a line's syllable length is the *verso piano*. This means that a line ending with a *tronco* word must, for the purposes of assessing line length, have a syllable added to it, while one ending with a *sdrucciolo* word must have a syllable subtracted from it. Thus "Le memorie d'un tempo che fù," which has nine syllables but ends with a *parola tronca*, is described as a kind of ten-syllable line, a *decasillabo tronco*. Similarly, "Suoni la tromba, e intrepido," which has eight syllables but ends with a *parola sdrucciola*, is described as a kind of seven-syllable line, a *settenario sdrucciolo*.

A further feature concerns the position of the main accents in the line. Lines with an equal number of syllables may differ according to the position of the main accents. The distinction is important in order to differentiate between *versi semplici* (simple lines) and *versi doppi* (double lines): a *verso doppio* is built from two shorter lines with identical accent structure. Thus "O Signore, dal tetto natìo" and "Vieni d'amore—in sen ripara" both contain ten syllables, but the first is a *decasillabo* (accents on the third, sixth, and ninth syllables) whereas the second is a *quinario doppio* (accents on the fourth and ninth syllables).

More terminology concerns the various rhyme schemes and broad groupings of types of verse. *Rima alternata* is *abab cdcd*; *rima baciata* is *aa bb cc dd*. In poetry for musical drama there is a clear distinction between *recitativo* and set "numbers" (arias, duets, choruses, ensembles). Whereas for the set numbers the structure of the poetic text is ruled by a principle of symmetry (they are built on two or more verses, all on the same type(s) of verse and rhyme scheme), the standard meter for *recitativo* is *verso sciolto*: *settenari* and *endecasillabi*, freely alternated without rhyme scheme except at the end of a section, which is usually marked by a *rima alternata* or *rima baciata*, with the last line usually a *verso tronco*.

MUSIC IN THE THEATER

INTRODUCTION

THIS VOLUME contains a series of essays whose primary subject is musical theater. More precisely: in the following pages facts and problems are centered around that strange, indeed unique, phenomenon of Western civilization in which drama, poetry, music, and spectacle join together to create what is generally known as opera. This term certainly refers to well-defined historical events; yet, at the same time, these essays are concerned with a live experience of our time. Most of the ideas and interpretations proposed in this book—whatever their value—were tested against a direct, emotional response in the opera house. What is more, the germ, the cell of many of the thoughts discussed here originated from the impact of a particularly striking and stimulating performance. This explains why, of all the possible questions that such a multiform and articulated cultural phenomenon may provoke, some return time and again, applied to composers from different historical periods and belonging to different cultural traditions. In short, musical theater is considered here as both a cultural document of the past and, at the same time, an immediate, direct, and contemporary artistic experience.

The fact that most of the essays contained in this book are devoted to the operas of Verdi should not mislead the reader. Long familiarity with this repertory offered, ready at hand, a set of well-known examples against which to test hypotheses and interpretations. Almost paradoxically, the historical context in which the composer was active facilitated my task. In the correspondence with his collaborators, Verdi was constantly at pains to explain, to clarify the intellectual principles that guided his activity; this was for him a necessity, given the distance between his conception of musical drama and the century-old tradition onto which it was being grafted. Verdi was obliged to verbalize what he wanted and why he wanted it that particular way. But Verdi had also to clarify (first of all to himself) how to handle the language of music, how to "bend" it, to make it an instrument of his intentions, of his dramatic conception. He had to test it, to struggle with it, until it assumed a shape that could manifest, in musical terms, his idea of musical theater: hence our need to study the composing process, as witnessed by the different sketches and by the variants in the autograph scores.

The fact that Verdi's output is at the center of this volume should not, therefore, limit my conclusions exclusively to that repertory. Rather, it should encourage the reader to apply them to the works of other opera composers, possibly those belonging to other historical moments. What I intend to present is a set of ideas, ones that can be understood as possible explanations of musico-dramatic events from different periods and different cultural traditions.

This book also illustrates the way in which these conclusions were reached, the intellectual process through which they were arrived at; it is the story of how some basic issues of musical theater became gradually clear to an author and how he tried to verify them. Indeed, the first task was to find out precisely what these issues were.

These essays were written over a long period of time: the oldest one dates from 1966, whereas others—although presented in public in the form of lectures—have until now remained unpublished. They are arranged in roughly chronological order, since the sequence reflects the step-by-step development and clarification of the thoughts that constitute the book's essence. Throughout runs the quest for an answer to fundamental questions, stimulated by the repertory on which it is based: why is it that only a few operas (and *those* operas, among thousands written before, at the same time, and afterward) constitute the standard repertory of all opera houses throughout the world, to the constant delight of their audiences? What makes these operas as effective today as they were at the time of their creation? Is there a governing principle in their organization and structure? And, if so, what is it? In order to answer these questions, I felt I had to identify the constituent elements of musico-dramatic discourse. As this process unfolded, new criteria and new intellectual methods were postulated by the results thus far acquired. The research was developed primarily through study of the operas themselves rather than through the evaluation of the so-called secondary sources. It was necessary to turn, and return, to the libretto, to the score—and to the opera house—in order to verify the hypotheses and test the results achieved; one had to depart from there, in order to acquire a deeper and more precise knowledge and understanding of those tantalizing and attractive objects. All this explains why I made little attempt, during this long and sometimes tormented journey, to compare my conclusions with those reached by other scholars along the same line of research. This holds true even for distinguished, internationally renowned authorities—such as, to mention only the most obvious name, Carl Dahlhaus. With the deepest admiration and respect for the work of this great German scholar, and at risk of sounding presumptuous and arrogant, I preferred to pursue the path I had opened up for myself and to develop my research and hypotheses independently.

The reader will immediately see that my taste in new analytical methods has been overtly catholic; it has been, at the same time, consciously cautious in the sense that new ways were approached only when the need to further explain available evidence demanded them. Instead of using these new intellectual tools in a systematic way, I chose a somewhat pragmatic approach. The important thing was to find an explanation rather than to prove a theory. All this book aims at is to clarify and to understand.

In the first essays, the most ubiquitous and frequently applied method in the field of historical musicology—comparison between a work and its possible models—was thoroughly exploited, the underlying principle being that the identification of similarities may reveal, *ex absentia*, what was peculiar to the work itself. Although this method is certainly fruitful when one wishes to establish the historical position of a work and the cultural perspective of its author, it unfortunately helps very little in identifying *what* constitutes its originality. The questioning had therefore to move in other directions. The study of the composing process proved to be a successful avenue: to determine the way in which—and the reason why—the composer, in his "workshop," reached certain musical decisions when he wanted to define a specific moment of the dramatic action. From the definition of a single episode or moment, my attention gradually shifted toward larger dramatic units: first single scenes, then a whole act; then, possibly, the entire opera. It had in fact become evident that the musical definition of a dramatically relevant detail generated a formal principle—or, rather, a unifying device—to be used, singled out with that function, throughout the score. In working out a dramatic detail, the composer reached a clearer vision of the overall shape of his work; he discovered how to organize it, by which musical means.

It was necessary then to move from the definition of a single dramatic moment to the general plan of the opera; the problem had become one of structure—not only of musical structure but also of other, related formal levels, indissolubly connected with the musical organization of the score. Furthermore, the composer's need to define the overall shape of the work, and to determine its unifying principles, was already present at the stage of the composing process and was thus contemporary with the defining of the musical language. It was necessary to identify the organization of the action on stage—why certain episodes rather than others were to be chosen from the literary text that is generally at the basis of the libretto; it was necessary to understand and to identify the organization of the dialogue in verses and stanzas and to find out why specific metrical and rhythmic poetic patterns were chosen.

But what had became absolutely clear, in the course of my research, was that what mattered above all was not so much the presence and the organization of each of these structures but their relationship to one another, the mutual influence of these three structural levels.

It may also happen that the composer was not concerned to establish a formal unifying principle in his score. This was clearly the case with Bellini, as my analysis of the making of *I puritani* reveals. But Bellini paid the greatest attention to the pace with which the action unfolds; rather than with the overall organization of his score, he was concerned with the variety and the balance between successive dramatic moments. In this way, another basic feature of musical theater became evident: dramatic rhythm, the rhythm created by the succession and alternation of the episodes. It is primarily through this alternation that the audience's attention is constantly maintained.

Indissolubly connected with the concept of dramatic rhythm is the musical duration of each episode, both in itself and in relation to the context in which it is placed. It was necessary to see how much time was needed in order to impress on the spectator's memory the characterizing elements of the musico-dramatic discourse.

Another fundamental element of musical theater had thus become clear: its temporal dimension. This principle, intuitively acquired and used by the great creators of the seventeenth- and eighteenth-century musical theater, became a conscious principle of dramatic organization with Gluck, as the essay on the opening scenes of *Alceste* tries to demonstrate. The most important consequence of Gluck's discovery lies in the new, broadened temporal dimension acquired by each dramatic episode; with Gluck, a new concept of musical (as well as dramatic) time was firmly established, one that was adopted and brought to its extreme consequences precisely by those composers who, in their writings, overtly expressed their admiration for and debt to Gluck: Berlioz and Wagner.

Strictly related to the principle of temporal dimension was the other aspect of the problem: the establishing of a musical connection between dramatically related moments of the action. Each composer found a solution peculiar to his musical language. From direct references, or quotations of musical ideas heard previously in the course of the action (what are usually called "recurring themes"), it was possible to identify the use of more elementary but, for this very reason, more subtle—and therefore susceptible to more refined dramatic articulation—musical means. The entire history of opera could be rewritten if considered from this point of view. As far as Verdi is concerned, his encounter with Shakespeare's theater—specifically, with *Macbeth*—led him to conceive a kind of organization that was in a sense a combination of two principles: pithy musical ideas—such as the motive connected with the words "Tutto è finito!"—and isolated elements of the musical language—like the timbre of the English horn, whose "solo" punctuates the opera. The way in which these two musical means were used throughout the score, especially the way in which they were elaborated and applied to different structural levels of organization, is a clear sign of their importance in the definition of the dramatic discourse. On the same level, the analysis of the dramatically characterizing elements of *Il trovatore* revealed that traditionally accepted stylistic differences are much less powerful when considered from this point of view; the musico-dramatic language of *Il trovatore* is the logical continuation and development of the principles Verdi discovered during his work on *Macbeth*.

When applied systematically to the analysis of an entire act, such as the first of *La forza del destino*, these principles help also to clarify the use—or drastic modification—of conventional formal organizations, such as that of nineteenth-century duet, and therefore allow us to specify the historical position of the composer at that moment of his creative activity. Musico-dramatic analysis and historical evaluation of specific art works seem in this way to complement each other.

Some of the ideas offered in the essays collected here seem to have stimulated other writers to discuss and challenge them and also to develop them in order to bring them to their logical conclusion; I would like to mention in particular the essays of Harold Powers,[1] Roger Parker,[2] William Drabkin,[3] and Fabrizio Della Seta.[4] I feel sincerely grateful to these colleagues for paying so much attention to my thoughts and privileged that they deemed it worthwhile to elaborate on them. I strongly advise the reader to consider their writings as complementary to mine, as an essential continuation and completion of the ideas expressed in the following pages.

Notes

1. Harold S. Powers, "'La solita forma' and 'The Uses of Convention,'" *Nuove prospettive nella ricerca verdiana.* (Atti del convegno internazionale in occasione della prima del "Rigoletto" in edizione critica) Vienna, 12–13 March 1983 (Parma/Milan, 1987), pp. 74–109; also in *Acta musicologica* 59 (1987): 65–90.

2. Roger Parker, "Levels of Motivic Definition in Verdi's *Ernani*," *19th-Century Music* 6 (1982): 141–50.

3. William Drabkin, "Characters, Key Relations, and Tonal Structure in *Il trovatore*," *Music Analysis* 1 (1983): 143–53.

4. Fabrizio Della Seta, "'O cieli azzurri': Exoticism and Dramatic Discourse in *Aida*," *Cambridge Opera Journal* 3, no. 1, 49–62.

CHAPTER 1

FROM ROSSINI'S *MOSÉ* TO VERDI'S *NABUCCO*

TO INTRODUCE *Nabucco*, to illustrate even a few of its musico-dramatic characteristics, entails comparison with preceding and contemporary operatic production: we need to define what in this opera is typical of Verdi's style, to distinguish what is *not* Verdian. We should not forget that even during the composer's lifetime *Nabucco* was regarded as his first "authentic" product. What is more, Verdi himself seems to have been of the same opinion: in the so-called Autobiographical Sketch narrated to Giulio Ricordi, he states that "with this opera [*Nabucco*] one could truly say that my artistic career began."[1]

However paradoxical it may seem, research on the earliest stages of Verdi's musico-dramatic style has hardly begun.[2] Apart from a few distinguished but isolated exceptions, the essential stylistic and musical components of Italian opera in the first forty years of the nineteenth century still await critical definition; and until such studies have been undertaken—studies that will have as their basis matters of musical style—it is hard to write with absolute certainty of *this* rather than *that* musico-dramatic characteristic in early Verdi.

The present essay, then, cannot offer anything like definitive conclusions; I simply wish to present some ideas that have emerged through a careful and—I hope—thoughtful reading of the opera with which Verdi began his triumphant ascent.

Even within these limitations, it may nevertheless be possible to establish some connections between *Nabucco* and earlier operas. It is always difficult to find incontrovertible proof of this kind of relationship—particularly in the case of Verdi; with *Nabucco* the situation is more-or-less hopeless, as we have almost no documents concerning the opera's origins or genesis: even the genesis of Verdi's first opera, *Oberto, conte di San Bonifacio*, is better documented. There is no mention of the birth of *Nabucco* in the *Copialettere* or in the four volumes of *Carteggi verdiani* edited by Alessandro Luzio;[3] nor has the collection of reproductions of Verdi's letters housed at the Istituto di studi verdiani in Parma so far produced anything of relevance.

We must, then, make do with what Verdi himself has told us, even though his accounts date from more than twenty-five years after the event. As it happens, the composer mentioned the early history of *Nabucco* more than once: we possess no less than three narratives, given on three separate occasions. The earliest was told to Michele Lessona during a conversation at Tabiano, a spa near Busseto, and was published by Lessona in his *Volere è potere* of 1869.[4] The second, extremely concise account is in a letter to Opprandino Arrivabene dated 7 March 1874 in which Verdi makes explicit mention of the Lessona version.[5] The third is in the so-called Autobiographical Sketch dictated to Giulio Ricordi on 19 October 1879 and published (with Verdi's consent, since we know that he read the proofs) in the Italian translation of Arthur Pougin's *Verdi, histoire anecdotique de sa vie et des ses oeuvres*.[6] How was it that Verdi, always so deeply reluctant to speak about himself, chose on three occasions to hold forth on a topic that involved both himself and his professional career, knowing full well that on at least two of these occasions what he said would be published? Undoubtedly the period during which *Nabucco* was created is *the* epic moment in the Verdian biography, the moment in which—with his triumph at La Scala—the composer's powerful personality asserted itself once and for all time on the public at large.[7]

The three narratives basically agree, except in a few minor but rather important details that we will examine later. But how far can we rely on them? Those scholars who have long wrestled with the problems of Verdian biography will know how adept the composer was at creating a public persona, at establishing a stereotyped portrait for a public always eager for details of his personal life; it was behind this self-made image that he tried to hide (indeed, succeeded in hiding) his true self, the one that we know today through such direct documentation as his correspondence with close relatives and trusted friends. It is, of course, precisely the absence of documentary evidence that forces us to accept—though with the greatest caution—what Verdi tells us; and this even though, for example, he ended the account to his trusted friend Opprandino Arrivabene with the words "Here then is my absolutely true story" (Eccoti la storia mia vera, vera, vera).[8]

After the disastrous reception of *Un giorno di regno* on 5 September 1840 Verdi, deeply wounded by its failure and by the recent death of his wife—a death that completed the destruction of his small family—decided to break the contract he had signed with the impresario at La Scala, Bartolomeo Merelli—a contract drawn up after *Oberto* that obliged the composer to write three further operas, the first of which had been *Un giorno di regno*. Thanks to the farsighted insistence of Merelli, the contract was not canceled: whenever Verdi wanted to have a new opera performed, he had merely to give the impresario the two months' notice needed to prepare the singers, scenery, and costumes. But Verdi wanted nothing more to do with music; he set about reading, as he said to Lessona, "terrible books, most of them those cheap novels [romanzacci] that were then so common in Milan."[9] Thus he spent the end of the autumn and beginning of winter 1841:

CHAPTER 1

I settled in Milan near the Corsia de' Servi: I had lost faith and thought no more of music, when one winter evening, coming out of the Galleria De Cristoforis, I run into Merelli, who was going to the theater. It was snowing in broad flakes, and taking me by the arm he invites me to accompany him to his office at La Scala. Along the way we chat, and he tells me he is in an awkward position about the new opera he must put on: he had given the assignment to Nicolai, but the latter was not satisfied with the libretto.

"Imagine!!" Merelli says, "a libretto by Solera, stupendous!!... Magnificent!!... Extraordinary!... Effective, grandiose dramatic situations! beautiful verses!... But that stubborn composer won't hear of it and declares it is an impossible libretto!... I am at a loss to find him another promptly."

"I'll solve your problem," I added. "Did you not have *Il proscritto* written for me? I have not written a note of it: I put it at your disposal."

"Oh! bravo... that is really good luck."

Saying this, we had reached the theatre: Merelli calls Bassi, the "poet," stage-director, call-boy, librarian, etc., etc., and tells him to look at once in the archive to see if he can find a copy of *Il proscritto*: the copy is there. But at the same time Merelli picks up another manuscript and, showing it to me, exclaims:

"Look, here is Solera's libretto! Such a beautiful subject, and to refuse it!... Take it... read it."

"What the devil am I to do with it?... No, no, I have no desire to read librettos."

"Oh, it won't do you any harm!... Read it and then bring it back to me." And he hands me the manuscript: it was a big script in broad letters, as was the custom then. I roll it up and, saying good evening to Merelli, I go off to my house.

Along the way I felt a kind of vague uneasiness, a supreme sadness, an anguish that swelled the heart!... I went home and with an almost violent gesture, I threw the manuscript on the table, stopping erect in front of it. Falling on the table, the sheaf opened on its own; without knowing how, my eyes stare at the page that lay before me, and this verse appears to me:

"Va, pensiero, sull'ali dorate..."

I glance over the following verses and I receive a deep impression from them, especially since they were almost a paraphrase of the Bible, which I always found pleasure in reading.

I read a passage, I read two: then, steadfast in my intention of not composing, I make an effort of will and force myself to close the script, and I go off to bed!... No good... *Nabucco* was trotting about in my head!... Sleep

> would not come: I get up and read the libretto, not once, but two, three times, so often that in the morning you could say that I knew Solera's entire libretto by heart.
>
> All the same I did not feel like going back on my decision, and during the day I return to the theatre and give the manuscript back to Merelli.
>
> "Beautiful, eh?...," he says to me.
>
> "Very beautiful."
>
> "Eh!... Then set it to music!..."
>
> "Not on your life.... I won't hear of it."
>
> "Set it to music, set it to music!..."
>
> And, saying this, he takes the libretto and jams it into the pocket of my overcoat, grabs me by the shoulders, and not only shoves me out of his office, but shuts the door in my face and turns the key.
>
> What to do?
>
> I returned home with *Nabucco* in my pocket: one day a verse, one day another, one time a note, another a phrase... little by little the opera was composed.[10]

The narrative Verdi told Lessona corresponds to this account even down to small details; but in the final part it differs in one significant respect. After Merelli has sent him off again with the libretto in his pocket,

> The young maestro returned home with his drama, but he threw it into a corner without a further glance, and for another five months carried on reading those bad novels.
>
> Then one fine day, at the end of May, he found himself with that blessed drama again in his hands: he reread the final scene, the death of Abigaille (the one that was later cut), sat down almost mechanically at the piano, the piano that had stood silent for so long, and composed the scene.
>
> The ice was broken [. . .] In three months from that time, *Nabucco* was composed, finished, precisely as it is today.[11]

There are various glosses one could make on this narrative, without moving too far away from the facts of the matter. First of all, what attracted Verdi in his reading of the libretto was the subject, and above all the biblical "tone," the imitation of that book he had "always found pleasure in reading" and the perusal of which he presumably alternated with those "cheap novels" he mentioned to Lessona. Another anecdote, again told by Verdi to Ricordi, underlines that this was the fundamental character the composer wanted to confer on the opera. During the writing of *Nabucco* Verdi, who had already made use of the librettist Temistocle Solera for alterations to *Oberto*, locked himself with the unwilling "poet" in a room in order to make him substitute a love duet between Ismaele and Fenena at the end of the third act with a "Profezia" for Zaccaria, the character whom, in a letter of 11 June 1843 to the bass Ignazio Marini, Verdi would define *tout court* as "Il Profeta."[12] To fashion the text of this blessed "Profezia" there was no need to look very far: "Here's the Bible, you have the words all ready-made," said Verdi to a dismayed Solera; and the change was made precisely to maintain (as Verdi said to Ricordi) "the biblical *grandeur* that characterized the drama."[13]

This is the only alteration to Solera's text that we know was undertaken on Verdi's instructions. However, there is little doubt (though only a comparison with the model used by Solera for his libretto could prove the matter) that the composer caused his librettist to make other changes, ones that we are not yet able to identify.

From Verdi's accounts of the origins of *Nabucco* it thus seems clear that the suffering of the Hebrew people, expressed in solemn, biblical terms, was the element that awoke and then held the composer's interest; but it is equally true (as the Lessona narrative tells us) that the composing of the opera began not with a grandiose choral passage but with the final scene, the death of Abigaille—the scene that was then cut from almost all subsequent nineteenth-century performances of the opera.

Around these two poles—a people dramatically fearful for their salvation and an unusual female figure who suppresses her femininity because of a thirst for power and revenge—Verdi constructed his score.

It is worth stressing again that, notwithstanding all his statements to the contrary, Verdi from the beginning saw very clearly the elements on which to build his musical edifice, the hinges around which the entire dramatic structure would pivot. It is the clarity with which he saw the fundamental themes and the precision with which they are realized musically that make it difficult to accept his statement to Giulio Ricordi that the opera was composed "one day a verse, one day another, one time a note, another a phrase," as if to say it was written haphazardly, during an indefinite period between January and the autumn of 1841. The Lessona account—that the opera was composed between the end of May and the end of August 1841, and that composition began with Abigaille's death scene—seems much more likely.

But what of this libretto, so emphatically praised by Merelli, but seeming to Nicolai "impossible" to set to music?

There are four "parts" (not acts), each with a title: "Gerusalemme" (Jerusalem), "L'empio" (The impious one), "La profezia" (The prophecy), and "L'idolo infranto" (The broken idol). Each carries as a subtitle a verse from the Book of Jeremiah (at least if we believe the captions beneath each of them: actually only the first and the fourth of these citations can be found in the Bible; the other two are vague paraphrases, rather than precise quotations, from Jeremiah). As is well known, the whole of Jeremiah hinges on the Israelites' captivity in Babylon; but this is not the only biblical passage that speaks of Nebuchadnezzar and the imprisonment in Babylon of the Hebrew people: chapters 24 and 25 of 2 Kings, chapter 36 of 2 Chronicles, the Book of Psalms, and above all the first four chapters of Daniel all contain accounts of the captivity. But none of these passsages contains anything more specific than the invasion of Judah by the king of Babylon, the captivity of the Iraelites, their being led in slavery, Nebucadnezzar's madness, prophesied by Daniel and caused by the king's pride; in both the opera and the Bible this madness is followed by a return to reason caused by the Assyrian king's offering a prayer to the God of Israel. If the events of the libretto give a very different impression from those of the Bible, the language, the images that the librettist made use of, are often directly biblical.

We can immediately see that the Zaccaria of the libretto is intended as a dramatic representation of the biblical Jeremiah, because there is a close parallel between the language of this character and the prophet's utterances in the Bible; and this is curious, since in the economy of Verdi's libretto Zaccaria has a very precise function and characterization, one that has nothing to do with that of Jeremiah, the biblical prophet.

Possible analogies with the Bible end here. All the other characters in the opera derive from Solera's imagination or are taken from earlier theatrical sources and are grafted—according to that process of "contamination" typical of the theatrical texts of any period—onto the biblical base.[14] It is clear that the principal source of Solera's libretto is a four-act play by Auguste Anicet-Bourgeois and Francis-Cornu, *Nabuchodonosor*, first performed in Paris at the Théâtre de l'Ambigu-Comique on 17 October 1836.[15] However, even though a comparison between the play and the libretto would be extremely revealing, the French *pièce* was not the only source that Solera (whether guided by Verdi or not) used in constructing his libretto; in any case, a sure link between the play and the libretto is a ballet on the same subject, and drawn from the same theatrical model, given at La Scala in autumn 1838.[16]

Next to the oppressed people we always find, as both comforter and animator, the "prophet" Zaccaria; as the enemy approaches in the first act, Zaccaria instructs the people to have faith in the Lord; in the third act, when the Hebrews lament their homeland "sì bella e perduta" on the banks of the Euphrates, Zaccaria consoles them by prophesying that Babylon will be destroyed by the power of the "Lion of Judah." I have already emphasized that this piece was written at the composer's explicit request to replace a love duet that he deemed inappropriate at that point. The composer strove then to achieve a specific characterization for Zaccaria, that of a comforting guide who rekindles in the hearts of the Hebrew exiles their spent faith.

This characterization is remarkably similar, in both the libretto and the score, to that of an earlier figure in nineteenth-century Italian opera: the protagonist of Rossini's *Mosé*. Mosé also reanimates through solemn declamation the Hebrew prisoners (this time, of the Egyptian pharaoh), exorts them to have faith in the Lord, and prays for them and with them. Mosé, like Zaccaria, is cast as a bass. Even an early commentator such as Abramo Basevi knew that Verdi was influenced by the Rossini opera during the composition of *Nabucco*, if only through the similarity of their biblical plots;[17] but it will be useful to take a close look at the external circumstances that enabled the twenty-eight-year-old composer from provincial Busseto to gain a knowledge of Rossini's mature masterpiece. The first, three-act version of Rossini's opera, entitled *Mosé in Egitto*, was written to a libretto by Andrea Leone Tottola for the Teatro San Carlo of Naples and was first performed there in spring 1818; the second version, which boasted an entirely new act (the first) as well as many other modifications, with a libretto expanded and freely translated into French by Balocchi and De Jouy, was first performed at the Paris Opéra in 1827. Given the young Verdi's biography, it seems inevitable that the composer knew the second rather than the first version of *Mosé*. And he knew it not simply through reading and studying the score but by attending performances: the revised *Mosé* was first performed at Milan's Teatro della Canobbiana on 30 June 1835 and was revived on 10 October of the same year at La Scala, in both cases with great success; and the opera was staged again at La Scala, for a total of twenty-two performances starting on 30 May 1840,[18] hardly a year before the composition of *Nabucco*. In all these Milanese performances the part of the protagonist was taken by Ignazio Marini who, according to Regli,[19] had made the part of Mosé something of a specialty, who had also been the first Oberto in *Oberto, conte di San Bonifacio*, and to whom Verdi had made known, in the letter of 11 June 1843 mentioned earlier,[20] that he had written parts in both *Nabucco* and *I Lombardi* in which the singer "would have great effect." The part in *Nabucco* was, of course, that of Zaccaria.[21]

The similarities between characters in *Mosé* and *Nabucco* do not end with Mosé and Zaccaria. Nabucco, a baritone, is the tyrannical enemy of the Hebrew people, as is Faraone, also a baritone, in the Rossini opera; *Mosé*'s Amenofi, tenor and the son of Faraone, is in love with the soprano Anaide, niece of Mosé, just as in *Nabucco* the Israelite tenor Ismaele loves the Babylonian soprano Fenena. The relationship of voices to characters in the two operas involves even minor roles: Osiride, high priest of Iside in *Mosé*, is a bass, as is the high priest of Baal in *Nabucco*; and the captain of the guards in *Nabucco*, the comprimario tenor Abdallo, finds a parallel in *Mosé*'s Aufide, head of the guards and Faraone's messenger, also the comprimario tenor. This series of parallels, in both character type and voice type, seems too close to be accidental. It may thus be extremely significant that in *Nabucco* Verdi retained a character such as Anna, described in the libretto as "Zaccaria's sister," who has no function in the plot and who sings almost exclusively in the ensembles (sustaining the highest part). For Anna is surely just a transposition of "Maria, sister of Mosé" in Rossini's opera, and has no dramatic function whatsoever in Verdi's opera.[22]

WE CAN NOW consider the extent to which these correspondences with *Mosé* can be extended to a musical level: to see how far Verdi used the Rossini model when creating his opera. The first and most important lesson that the young Verdi drew from *Mosé* concerned the general "tone" of his score: the broad solemnity that Basevi characterized as "grandiose";[23] the "biblical *grandeur*" that, in Verdi's own words, "characterized the drama." To establish this tone, Verdi condensed into a single musical "number" two or more scenes of the libretto, thus focusing the essential ingredients of the plot and ignoring or downplaying secondary elements.

The opening scenes of the two operas (examples 1.1 and 1.2) offer a fine example of precisely how Verdi followed the Rossini model. The situation is the same: the Iraelites, afflicted by misfortune, are comforted and reanimated by the voice of the high priest, the "prophet." In both operas[24] a broad choral passage in minor (F minor in *Mosé*, E minor in *Nabucco*) immediately creates a sense of the desolation in which the chosen people are suffering. From the episode for full chorus[25] we move, with a modulation to the relative major (A♭ major in *Mosé*, G major in *Nabucco*) to a developmental passage (examples 1.3 and 1.4) in which new thematic material is presented by the male chorus. The structural correspondence between the two operas could hardly be more exact.

At this point Verdi broke from his model, but in such a way that we can still recognize the derivation. In *Mosé*, the female chorus repeats almost exactly the passage sung by the men, with only slight variations in harmony and orchestral accompaniment (example 1.5). Verdi found another solution: although he also used the female chorus, he gave it completely different thematic material, almost in contrast to the male chorus's music (example 1.6). The tonality is E major, and the orchestration is completely different. The repetition and development by the full chorus of this musical idea, first sung by the "Vergini," brings Verdi to the close of the first musical number of his score.

In *Mosé*, once the choral episode has finished, three chords on the low brass herald the entrance of the protagonist. The declamation on a single pitch, to a rhythm that marks the prosodic accents of the text, serves to highlight his spiritual character (example 1.7a): Mosé is the leader, the guide that gives strength to the people, whom he joins in suffering. The second part of this recitative again takes up the second part of the opening choral section (example 1.7b). Verdi employs the same type of declamation in Zaccaria's "Recitativo," yet again establishing a correspondence both of structure and of vocal style between the two operas (example 1.8).

The final part of *Mosé*'s opening scene unfolds according to a simple, neat scheme: the chorus replies to Mosé's exhortations by repeating, this time in F major, the phrase that had earlier been introduced by the male and then the female chorus; Mosé, joining his people with an encouraging gesture, repeats this passage and then introduces a new, more brilliant idea—one we already

EXAMPLE 1.1

Coro di Ebrei e Madianiti
Soprani 1.mi
Soprani 2.di e 3.zi
Tenori
Bassi
Ah! dell' em - pio al po -
te - re fe - ro - ce

EXAMPLE 1.1, *cont.*

EXAMPLE 1.2

Soprani
Tenori
Bassi
Ebrei, Leviti e Vergini Ebree
Gli ar - re - di fe - sti - vi giù ca - da - no in-
fran - ti, il po - pol di Giu - da di lut - to s'am-

Example 1.2, *cont.*

Example 1.3

p
Tenori
sotto voce
Coro
Ma chi pe - gno è al - la
Bassi
sotto voce
Ma chi pe - gno è al - la
spe - me tut - to - ra? Un cru - del senz' o -
spe - me tut - to - ra? Un cru - del senz' o -

EXAMPLE 1.3, *cont.*

EXAMPLE 1.4

know from the overture but that here assumes the function of an exhortation to have faith in God. The people reply to this invitation: the male chorus develops and rounds off the idea introduced by Mosé; the protagonist again repeats the first part of the phrase, which is this time completed by the female chorus; and the episode ends with a tutti in which the Iraelites again express their happy, simple confidence in the guidance God has offered them.

The same process of "persuasion" that we see in *Mosé* occurs in a much more elementary, less subtly refined form in *Nabucco*. Zaccaria's cantabile, "D'Egitto là sui lidi," exhorts his people to have faith in God; and evidently Zaccaria was for Verdi a more powerful orator than Mosé, because the entire musical period is immediately taken up and repeated by the full chorus, who thus answer enthusiastically the invitation of their leader.

EXAMPLE 1.5

At this point Ismaele's entry announcing the arrival of the king of Assyria should have shifted the musical and scenic action to a completely different level; but in order not to distract the audience from the atmosphere he has so clearly established, Verdi reduced the episode to a simple "bridge" in free style, with the principal part again falling to Zaccaria. The harmonic motion impels the episode forward, and eventually it explodes into the cabaletta, "Come notte a sol fulgente," in which the chorus once again repeats and echoes the voice of the prophet.

What Verdi derived from Rossini, then, was the tone of the musical language, and above all the structural organization of those ideas to which his teeming imagination, stimulated by his reading of the libretto, had given birth. His

Example 1.6

Vergini

p

Gran Nu - me, che vo - li sul -

V.

l'a - le dei ven - ti,

EXAMPLE 1.7a

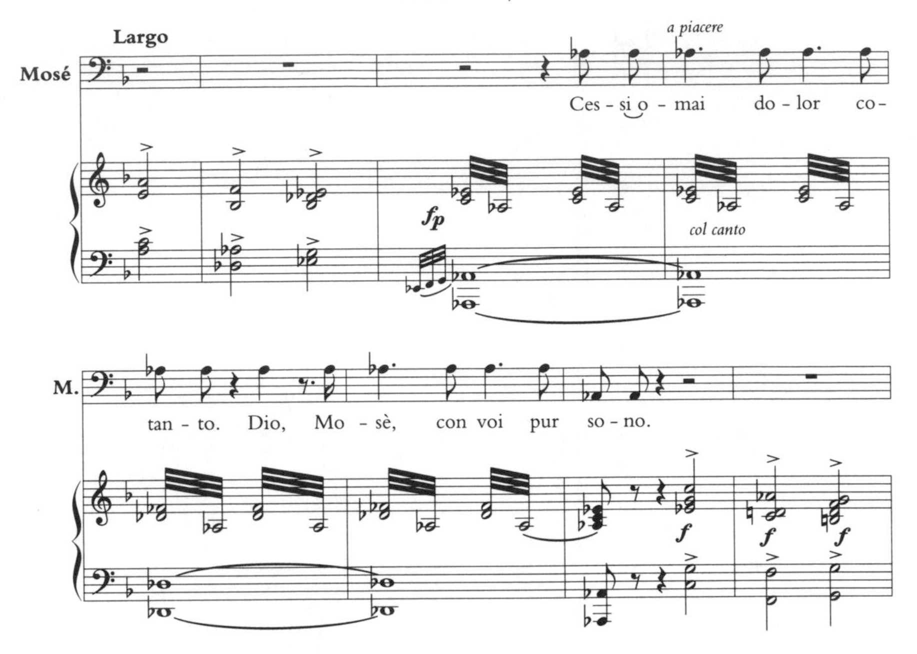

EXAMPLE 1.7b

Example 1.8

organization of the scene, however, was more independent and concentrated the audience's attention on the fundamental elements of the plot.

We can again trace to Rossini, and to *Mosé*, the sense of simple grandeur that Verdi conferred on the score. Verdi made use of musical motives that he then recalled in connection with specific characters, without however allowing them to assume a "programmatic" function: there is no systematic or logically articulated use of "themes," certainly no sense of a Wagnerian system of *Leitmotiven*. There are, rather, certain fixed points through which the audience immediately recognizes the return of a given situation.[26]

Once these motives are identified, it is easy to understand how the entire overture to *Nabucco* was composed *a posteriori*, from ideas in the score[27] developed under the influence of Rossini: we need think only of the "crescendo" built on a theme from the first-act finale. The entwining of these motives in the overture has no dramatic significance; it is merely an instrumental piece, ably built on those musical ideas that best lend themselves to juxtaposition, and drawing maximum effect from their contrast. With only one exception, all the motives in the overture are from choral passages in the opera: yet another indication that Verdi's real protagonist in *Nabucco* is the chorus.

And it is precisely in a choral number, in the opera's most famous piece, that Verdi broke decisively from the Rossinian model and, almost imperiously, spoke with his own voice—in a tone and through language that, if I am not mistaken, no one had assumed before him. I refer, of course, to "Va pensiero," a piece still perhaps not fully understood because its musical form has not been sufficiently considered. Even with this chorus there is a suggestion that Verdi initially looked at *Mosé*, more precisely at the equally celebrated "Preghiera" that constitutes the penultimate musical number of Rossini's score.[28] A comparison of the opening orchestral bars makes the case clear; the rhythmic similarities and shared dynamic contrast (i.e., the chords repeated in triplet or sextuplet groups, first piano, then forte) speak for themselves (examples 1.9a and 1.9b). However, the two passages—Rossini's "Preghiera" and Verdi's chorus—are very different in structure.

Example 1.9a

Example 1.9b

The "Preghiera" from *Mosé* consists basically of a single melodic phrase, first sung by the soloist in G minor, then leading in a very simple modulatory passage to the relative major, B♭. Starting in this key, the phrase is repeated by the chorus—in rhythmic but not melodic unison—and, with a similar modulatory movement, returns to the initial key, G minor.[29] This phrase is repeated three times, the only variation being in the solo part, which is given to the bass, then the tenor, and then the mezzo-soprano. Finally the passage is repeated in its entirety by the soloists and full chorus, in G major. Rossini's procedure is that of repetition articulated by different vocal colors; it is basically the same principle (though with different forces) used in the "crescendo"; in the "Preghiera" from *Mosé* there is no musical development, merely a strophic repetition of the initial period—albeit one that is impressively effective.

In "Va pensiero" there are no soloists; the entire episode is sung by the chorus. However, apart from certain particular moments, the chorus sings a single melodic line, exactly as if a soloist were performing an aria. This is Verdi's principal novelty: "Va pensiero" *is not a chorus but an aria given to the chorus*, and the typical form of an aria is present in all its characteristics.[30]

Luigi Dallapiccola has demonstrated the existence in nineteenth-century Italian opera of a traditional method of setting to music the four-line verse, or quatrain.[31] According to this method, the first and second lines define the fundamental "affect" of the strophe; but "the drama occurs in the third line." As Dallapiccola says, "this third line represents the culmination of musical tension, the peak of the emotional crescendo"; in short, the moment of truth. The fourth line then serves to round off the tension created in the third. Dallapiccola further demonstrated how this structural pattern, found in many Verdi arias, ariosos, and cavatinas, was also applied to much larger musical episodes, even to entire scenes; and he "discovered" this in a fascinating graph of the second-act terzetto in *Un ballo in maschera*.

The poetic text of the *Nabucco* chorus consists of four quatrains of *decasillabi*, with a *tronco* accent on each fourth line, to mark the quatrain's end:

Va pensiero sull'ali dorate,
Va ti posa sui clivi, sui colli
Ove olezzano libere e molli
L'aure dolci del suolo natal!
Del Giordano le rive saluta,
Di Sionne le torri atterrate . . .
Oh mia patria sì bella e perduta!
Oh membranza sì cara e fatal!
Arpa d'or dei fatidici vati
Perchè muta dal salice pendi?
Le memorie nel petto raccendi,
Ci favella del tempo che fu!

O simile di Solima ai fati
Traggi un suono di crudo lamento,
O t'ispiri il Signore un concento
Che ne infonda al patire virtù![32]

[Go, thoughts, on wings of gold;
Go, settle on the slopes, on the hills,
Where, soft and mild, the gentle breezes
Of our native soil are fragrant!
Salute the banks of the Jordan,
The toppled towers of Zion.
Oh my homeland so beautiful and lost!
Oh remembrance so dear and fateful!
Golden harp of the prophetic bards,
Why do you hang mute from the willow?
Rekindle memories in our breasts,
Tell us of times past!
Mindful of the fate of Jerusalem,
Draw forth a sound of bitter lamentation,
Or let the Lord inspire us with a melody
That will infuse our sufferings with strength!]

Even when read carefully, these lines do not seem to offer an organization that allows one single thought, one emotional attitude, to take precedence over others. The text is a paraphrase of "Super flumina Babylonis," Psalm 136 according to the Vulgate,[33] and is an expression of longing for the distant homeland. It must, then, be in the musical setting that we will find its most authentic sense.

The first strophe, in the home key of F♯ major, establishes with remarkable immediacy the melody's basic range and formal characteristics, its sentimental atmosphere. Something begins to move at the beginning of the second quatrain: with the first two lines we have a shift to the dominant of the main key, C♯ major; the tension increases on the third line, on the words "O mia patria sì bella e perduta," with a significant return to the opening key and melodic phrase: it is this passionate exclamation that sums up and sets a seal on this exposition of the piece's character and significance.

With the third quatrain we reach the climax: the voices no longer sing in unison but take different notes of the chord; the entire musical phrase unfolds in the dominant, C♯ major; the instrumental accompaniment is reinforced by the addition of winds; the voices enter forte and at the reprise—that is, on the third(!) line of the quatrain—fortissimo, reaching with the sopranos' E♯ the highest vocal pitch of the entire piece. The tension is at its greatest on the first and third lines of this third quatrain and is placed in even greater relief by the pianissimi and the prevelance of dissonances on the second and fourth lines. It is the culmination of the chorus, the moment that seems to define its identity. Verdi, the composer, felt part of the tragedy of a people in slavery, identified his music with the "arpa d'or" (golden harp), the lyre of the Psalm; his musical imagination became one with those patriotic aspirations that even then he undoubtedly felt passionately.

With the final quatrain we return to pianissimo and to an orchestral accompaniment consisting partly of solo instrumental "voices"; and, with the third line (yet again!), there is a reprise of the initial phrase in the tonic, with the chorus in unison.

The final line of the fourth quatrain, in contrast to all the others, is repeated; and the reason for this repetition lies in the need for structural balance. In "Va pensiero" thirty-six measures are given to the chorus; and it is on the seventeenth measure, exactly halfway through, that we find the point of maximum tension, the invocation of the "arpa d'or," the moment earlier termed one of "identity." This justly famous chorus therefore unfolds by describing a perfect arch.

In the preceding discussion, I have of course mentioned just one of the two fundamental aspects on which Verdi constructed his score; I have not, that is, made any reference to the dominating character of Abigaille. But at least one point should be made: in portraying this character, Verdi employed the same "abridged style" that he had used at the beginning of the opera to fashion the drama of the Hebrew people and the figure of their prophet, Zaccaria. Alone among the characters of *Nabucco*, there exists no parallel for Abigaille in *Mosè*. Abigaille possesses the first true female emotions delineated by Verdi, and this musical realization impressively prefigured some aspects of his mature style. In the dramatic representation of the captivity of the Hebrew people, and in the figure of Abigaille, Verdi made *Nabucco* an opera still vividly alive, still capable of directly affecting our emotions.

Postscript

The date of this essay (1966) justifies some drastic statements it contains about the auroral state of research on early Verdi operas. Since then, the field has been at the center of several important studies. I will limit myself here to those concerning the operas around and before *Nabucco*:

Julian Budden, *The Operas of Verdi*, vol. 1 (London, 1973), esp. 90–112;

Roger Parker, *Studies in Early Verdi (1832–1844)*, Ph.D. dissertation, University of London, 1981; reprinted in the Garland series *British Music Theses*, ed. John Caldwell (New York, 1989);

Paola Giovanelli, "La storia e la favola dell'*Oberto*," *Studi verdiani* 2 (1983): 38–58;

David Lawton and David Rosen, "Verdi's Non-Definitive Revisions: The Early Operas," in *Atti del III° congresso internazionale di studi verdiani* (Parma, 1974), 189–237;

Markus Engelhart, *Die Chöre in den frühen Opern Giuseppe Verdis* (Tutzing, 1988); *Verdi und andere—"Un giorno di regno," "Ernani," "Attila," "Il corsaro" in Mehrfachvertonungen* (Parma, 1992).

As far as *Nabucco* is concerned, the most important publication in recent years has been the new critical edition of the opera: *Nabucodonosor*, ed. Roger Parker, series 1, vol. 3 of *The Works of Giuseppe Verdi* (Chicago and Milan, 1987). In light of information uncovered by the edition and by other scholars, I should like to make the following annotations:

1. In the anecdote concerning Solera (see p. 11–12), Verdi does actually say that the substituted piece was Zaccaria's "Profezia" in Act III. But, as Julian Budden and Roger Parker have both pointed out, it is likely that Verdi's memory was faulty. The "grand pas de deux" for Fenena and Ismaele in the Cortesi ballet occurs after Abigaille's solo at the beginning of Act II, and so in the place now occupied by Zaccaria's "Preghiera"; and, for various reasons of manuscript structure, it is highly unlikely that the "Profezia" was a late addition, whereas it is quite possible that the "Preghiera" was.
2. Apropos of the cutting of Abigaille's death scene (see p. 11), the critical edition lists six libretti in which the death scene was included (from a total of some eighty consulted). They are from Brescia (1843), Lisbon (1843), Padua (1843), Trieste (1843), Bergamo (1843–44), and Mantua (1843–44).
3. For the exact origin of the quotations that preface each "part" of the libretto (see p. 12), see the introduction to the critical edition, xiii, n. 18.
4. In relation to what I say on p. 25, readers may like to consult Joseph Kerman's article "Verdi's Use of Recurring Themes," in Harold S. Powers, ed., *Studies in Music History: Essays for Oliver Strunk* (Princeton, 1968), 495–510.

Notes

1. This narrative was printed for the first time as an appendix to the sixth chapter of Arthur Pougin, *Giuseppe Verdi—Vita aneddotica, . . . con note ed aggiunte di Folchetto* [J. Caponi] (Milan, 1881), 40–46; this quotation is from p. 46.

2. See the postscript to the present chapter.

3. Gaetano Cesari and Alessandro Luzio, eds., *I copialettere di Giuseppe Verdi* (Milan, 1913); and Alessandro Luzio, ed., *Carteggi verdiani*, 4 vols. (Rome, 1935–47).

4. Michele Lessona, *Volere è potere* (Florence, 1869), 296–98; Lessona's entire ninth chapter (pp. 287–307) is devoted to Verdi.

5. Published in Annibale Alberti, ed., *Verdi intimo. Carteggio di Giuseppe Verdi con Il Conte Opprandino Arrivabene (1861–1886)* (Verona, 1931), 166–76.

6. This is the appendix cited in n. 1. Verdi's reading of the proofs is mentioned in Frank Walker, *The Man Verdi* (London, 1962; reprint, Chicago, 1982), 33.

7. To give an idea of *Nabucco*'s success, it will perhaps be useful to cite some revivals of the opera during its first six years; the documentation comes in part from Alfred Loewenberg, *Annals of Opera*, 2d ed. (Geneva, 1955), vol. 1, cols. 818–20; from Pompeo Cambiasi, *La Scala—1778–1889—Note storiche e statistiche*, 5th ed. (Milan, [1889]); from Walker, *The Man Verdi*, 174; and in part from printed libretti. It will be obvious that the list has no claims to completeness.

The first performance took place on 9 March 1842, and there were eight perfomances before the end of the season; from 13 August to December of the same year the opera was revived at La Scala and played no less than sixty-seven times; *Nabucco* was then performed at Venice (Teatro La Fenice) for the Carnival season 1842–43, at Piacenza (Teatro Comunitativo) in spring 1843; at Vienna, for the first time outside Italy, on 4 April and at Parma (Teatro Ducale) on 17 April of that year; it was given at Bologna (Teatro Comunale) on 8 October, at Turin (Teatro Carignano), Cagliari, and Lisbon in the autumn of 1843; at Verona (Teatro Filarmonico) on 10 January 1844, at Florence (Teatro della Pergola) for the Carnival season, at Rovereto (Teatro Sociale) in the spring, and at Barcelona on 2 May 1844; again in 1844, the opera was performed in the summer at Lucca (Teatro del Giglio) and at Siena (Teatro dei Rinnovati), in the autumn at Leghorn (Teatro Rossini), Corfù (Teatro S. Giacomo), Malta, Berlin, and Stuttgart (for the first time in German); still in 1844, though we are not sure of the season, performances were held in Portugal at Porto (Teatro de S. Joao). The opera was revived at Marseilles and in Algier in summer 1845, at Alessandria on 25 October, at Paris and Hamburg in the autumn of that year; at Modena on 11 January 1846, at Cremona (Teatro della Concordia) and Copenhagen in the Carnival of 1846, at London (as *Nino*, at Her Majesty's Theatre) on 3 March 1846, at Budapest in the summer and at Constantinople in the autumn of that year, at Havana, again at Budapest (but this time in Hungarian) and Bucharest in 1847, at New York and Brussels in 1848; all this without mentioning revivals at these and other cities. See also the postscript to this chapter.

8. Alberti, *Verdi intimo*, 176.

9. Lessona, *Volere è potere*, 296.

10. Pougin, *Vita aneddotica*, 43–45; the English translation (with a few alterations) is from William Weaver, *Verdi: A Documentary Study* (London, n.d.), 13.

11. Lessona, *Volere è potere*, 297–98.

12. The autograph of this letter is in Venice, at the Biblioteca del Conservatorio "Benedetto Marcello." It is published in *I copialettere* (see n. 3), 423.

13. Pougin, *Vita aneddotica*, 45; italics mine.

14. This is even true of Ismaele, since there seems to be no connection between any biblical Ishmael and "Ismaele, nephew of Sedecia, the king of Jerusalem," who is the tenor in Verdi's opera.

15. The title page reads: "NABUCHODONOSOR, drame en quatre acts, Par MM. Anicet Bourgeois et Francis-Cornu, décors de Mm. Philestre et Cambon, mise en scène de M. Grandville, musique de M. Chautagne, répresenté pour la première fois, a Paris, sur le Théâtre de l'Ambigu-Comique, le 17 octobre 1836," published in *Magasin Théâtral* . . . , vol. 14 (Paris, 1836).

16. "NABUCCODONOSOR [*sic*], Ballo Storico in 5 parti composto e diretto da Antonio Cortesi da rappresentarsi nell'I. R. Teatro alla Scala l'autunno del 1838. Milano, Gaspare Truffi, MDCCCXXXVIII." (A copy is found in the Biblioteca Livia Simoni of the Museo Teatrale alla Scala.) The "avvertimento" clearly states the French play as the ballet's source: "In this fruit of my long labor, based on a French Drama that has made a sensation in Paris, and that has recently been translated by the learned signor G., I have moved the setting from Babylon to Jerusalem [. . .]." The ballet's succession of events follows for the most part those in Solera's libretto.

17. Abramo Basevi, *Studio sulle opere di Giuseppe Verdi* (Florence, 1859), 1–18, esp. p. 1.

18. Cambiasi, *La Scala* (see n. 7), 278, 282, 368.

19. Francesco Regli, *Dizionario biografico dei più celebri poeti ed artisti melodrammatici, tragici e comici* . . . (Turin, 1860), 308, s.v. MARINI Ignazio: "[. . .] He sang at La Scala, Milan for many years; his *Mustafà* and his *Mosé* will not easily be forgotten [. . .]."

20. See n. 12.

21. Curiously, in the numerous libretti of *Nabucco* that I consulted, I fail to find a single occasion on which Ignazio Marini sang the part of Zaccaria.

22. Neither in the French play by Anicet-Bourgeois and Francis-Cornu nor in the Cortesi ballet does there appear a female character with the name Anna, sister of Zaccaria; apart from this exception, all the ballet's characters correspond in name to those of Verdi's opera.

23. Basevi, *Studio sulle opere*, 4.

24. For the musical examples from *Mosé* I have used the following vocal score: G. Rossini, *Mosè*. Melodramma sacro in quattro atti di Stefano de Jouy . . . Milano-Roma-Napoli, G. Ricordi & C., pl. no. 44109.

25. Verdi was particularly struck by the rhythmic cell 𝅘𝅥𝅯𝅘𝅥.. 𝅘𝅥𝅯𝅘𝅥

26. See the postscript to the present chapter.

27. Below is a formal scheme of the overture, indicating the corresponding passage in the opera (part, scene, and musical "number"); for the central section of the sinfonia, "Allegro," **c**, I make use of the rehearsal letters that accompany the Ricordi vocal score "A cura di Mario Parenti" (1963):

Andante **c**. There is no direct derivation; there are however clear similarities with Part I, scene 1, "Coro d'introduzione" (at the words "Deh! l'empio non gridi, con baldo blasfèma");
Allegro **c**. Part II, scene 4, "Coro di Leviti" ("Il maledetto—non ha fratelli");
Andantino 3/8. Part III, scene 4, "Coro di Schiavi Ebrei" ("Va pensiero")—note that in the opera the meter is **c**;
Allegro. Again Part II, scene 4, "Coro di Leviti" ("Il maledetto—non ha fratelli"); then:
At letter C. Part II, scene 2, "Coro di Magi" ("Noi già sparso abbiamo fama");
At letter D. Part I, scene 7, "Stretta del 1° Finale" ("Dalle genti sii rejetto");
At letter F. Part III, scene 3, "Duetto" (orchestral accompaniment to the words "Egro giacevi . . . Il popolo");
At letter G. reprise of Part II, scene 2, "Coro di Magi";
At letter H. reprise of Part I, scene 7, "Stretta del 1° Finale";
Più stretto. Reprise in major of Part II, scene 4, "Coro di Leviti."

28. Notice also that the number preceding the finale of Part IV in *Nabucco* is Fenena's "Preghiera."

29. In order to follow clearly the ensuing discussion, the reader is invited to have at hand the vocal scores of Rossini's "Preghiera" and Verdi's "Va pensiero."

30. Rossini was well aware of this: he described the chorus as "a grand aria sung by sopranos, contraltos, tenors, and basses" (quoted by Carlo Gatti, *Verdi* [Milan, 1931], 207, without, however, a source for the quotation).

31. Luigi Dallapiccola, "Parole e musica nel melodramma," in *Quaderni della Rassegna musicale*, vol. 2 ("L'opera di Luigi Dallapiccola") (Turin, 1965), 117–39 reprinted several times in Italian and finally in L. Dallapiccola, *Parole e musica*, ed. Fiamma Nicolodi (Milan, 1980), 66–93; English translation: "Words and Music in Italian Nineteenth-Century Opera," in William Weaver and Martin Chusid, eds., *The Verdi Companion* (New York, 1979), 193–215; also in Rodney Shackelford, ed., *Dallapiccola on Opera* (n.p., Toccata Press, 1987), 133–63.

32. I take the text from the libretto of the first performance at La Scala: NABUCODONOSOR / Dramma lirico / in quattro parti / di / Temistocle Solera / da rappresentarsi nell'I. R. Teatro alla Scala / il carnevale 1842. Milan, Per Gaspare Truffi MDCCCXLII (p. 26).

33. The paraphrase was deliberate. As Lessona reports: "[Verdi] immediately felt the biblical *Super flumina Babylonis* [. . .]," Lessona, *Volere è potere*, 297.

CHAPTER 2

VERDI AND *DON GIOVANNI*: ON THE OPENING SCENE OF *RIGOLETTO*

By GENERAL agreement, *Rigoletto* is the first work of Verdi's artistic maturity, the opera in which he fully realized for the first time his musico-dramatic conception, in which a Verdian "style" (in the broadest sense of that term) finally came into its own and assumed its true features.

All this meant a break, a sense of distance (gradually established but nonetheless noticeable) from all previous operatic production—not only Verdi's but also those of his contemporaries. This leap forward has been examined from a dramatic standpoint by others: a clear definition of the characters, for example, closely linked in this opera to the development of the plot. Less often discussed—in fact mentioned only in brief asides and isolated analyses—are the specifically musical aspects of this Verdian "revolution": the musical means Verdi employed to bring his dramatic conception fully to life; how he dealt musically with problems of characterization, of differentiation between the various characters; through which musical means he made manifest the unfolding of the plot.[1]

In my opinion, this "revolution" in style coincided with Verdi's becoming aware that he needed to organize the entire dramatic structure on a corresponding musical level. He wrote explicity of the need for such a unitary conception: "In order to write well one needs to write as if in a single breath, leaving time later to adjust, to dress up, to polish the general sketch; without this, one risks producing an opera with frequent long breaks [*a lunghi intervalli*], with mosaic music, devoid of style and character."[2]

It is clear, then, that the stylistic elements available to the composer had of necessity to be broadened: they were insufficient to characterize musically (i.e., in terms of the musical dialectic) the entire unfolding of the plot. The musical tradition within which Verdi's early works were embedded—a tradition represented by the works of Rossini, Donizetti, and Bellini—offered no more than a partial solution to such a wide-ranging problem. And so Verdi turned to a non-Italian operatic tradition to which he felt connected by taste and temperament: to Meyerbeer, and to a "classical" past that was even at the time regarded as synonymous with absolute formal perfection—Mozart. Once he had found the solution to this problem—that of adapting his musical language to the demands of the dramatic conception—the new acquisitions become an integral part of his style, of the dialectics of his musical drama.

The example that I should like to offer as an illustration seems particularly clear: it betrays its terms of reference in an obvious manner—but there is little doubt that more detailed and searching inquiries would offer further discoveries.

THE AMBIENCE within which *Rigoletto* unfolds is the duke of Mantua's court; as in the play on which it was based, Victor Hugo's *Le Roi s'amuse*, Triboulet's tragedy takes place at the court of Francis I. Hugo well knew that nothing could depict better the frivolous, corrupt, and at the same time elegant atmosphere of the king of France's court, as he imagined it, than to begin the drama in the midst of a feast: a grand party at the court of a licentious, absolute ruler. Verdi likewise fully understood the need for this immediate characterization of ambience; and he also knew that the duke's licentiousness was an essential element of the plot. In a famous letter of 14 December 1850 to Marzari, president of the Teatro La Fenice in Venice, Verdi discussed some changes to the libretto that had been requested by the censors:

> If the names had to be changed, then the locality must also be changed, and so have a prince, a duke of another country, for example a Pier Luigi Farnese or some other, or else put the action back before Louis XI when France was not yet united, and have a duke of Burgundy, or of Normandy, etc., etc. At any rate an absolute ruler [. . .]. The old man's curse, so terrible and sublime in the original, here becomes ridiculous [. . .]. Without this curse what purpose, what meaning does the drama have? The duke becomes a noncharacter: the duke must absolutely be a rake; without that one cannot justify Triboletto's fear that his daughter come out of her hiding place, without that this drama is impossible.

And, a few lines farther on: "[. . .] I say frankly that my music, whether beautiful or ugly, is not written haphazardly and that I always strive to give it character."[3]

A grand party at the court of a libertine, a "young and extremely licentious cavalier": to create this atmosphere there was a model ready at hand—the final scene of *Don Giovanni*, Act I. And it was to this scene that Verdi turned in order to construct the opening of his drama, to create in the audience a well-defined impression of the physical and—above all—moral atmosphere within which the plot was to unfold, to give the duke that aspect of licentiousness without which he would have been a "noncharacter." The simplest, most basic musical means that a composer can use to create a festive atmosphere are dance tunes and rhythms. In the Mozart model three onstage orchestras play simultaneously, entering one after another in constrasting rhythms. Mozart used this procedure to raise the tension to its maximum, to create a "crescendo" of emotional response that is finally interrupted by Zerlina's offstage cry. This is the moment in which the rake reveals his true nature, and it is the concluding scene in the exposition of the drama. In *Rigoletto*, on the other hand, the parallel episode occurs at the beginning of an act, in fact at the beginning of the entire action. As a consequence, the three rhythms and the three instrumental groups are not superimposed; instead, they alternate in order to depict the ambience, create its atmosphere; in comparison to *Don Giovanni*, they are dramatically at the opposite pole.

The three dance movements are, then, the basic element, the framework that will characterize the duke's court; and thus they introduce the duke himself, who is its absolute ruler. Various dialogues are inserted into this musical continuum, and the duke's own Ballata emerges seamlessly from it. The basic musical framework is already present in Verdi's sketch of *Rigoletto*:[4] in this initial section, the vocal parts are for the most part merely hinted at (and are often different from the definitive version); but the first eight measures of both the opening dance and the Minuetto are fully notated, with all accompanying parts. The presence of the inner voices is especially significant in that the harmony of these dance movements is extremely simple: Verdi's usual habit was to notate harmony in his sketch only at the most complex or most dramatically significant points.

But the affinity between the Mozart and Verdi scenes is not merely structural. The simultaneity of the three dances in Mozart explains why they are all in the same key, G major, whereas in Verdi the first two dances are in A♭ major and the third in C major. There are no thematic or rhythmic affinities with Mozart's score in the first of Verdi's dances, which is in common time and played by the banda, a fact that perhaps explains Abramo Basevi's comment on the passage: "[. . .] we hear some lively dance music, in the second part of which there begins a *staccato* melody such as *Verdi* loves, models of which are frequent in the most recent dance music from Germany" (see example 2.1a).[5] The relationship between the first dance in *Don Giovanni* and the Minuetto in *Rigoletto* (examples 2.1a and 2.1b), on the other hand, is close enough to be taken as a quotation; Verdi eliminates Mozart's two oboes and two horns but continues the imitation even to the point of using the same figuration of arpeggiated sixteenth-notes (found in the second part of the Mozart minuet) for the accompaniment of the reprise of the theme.

The Perigordino, the third dance in *Rigoletto*, resembles in some respects the third dance in *Don Giovanni*: at least both are in compound time—3/8 in Mozart, 6/8 in Verdi. We might note in passing that in the *Rigoletto* sketch this dance (example 2.2) was in F major and had a melodic idea different from that of the definitive version, even though they share the same meter. Unlike the other two dances, no harmony was notated in the sketch.

Once it entered Verdi's musical vocabulary, the idea of having small instrumental groups on stage, performing dance rhythms in order to characterize a festive atmosphere, proved long-lasting. One need think no farther than the first act of *La traviata*, in which the offstage waltz following the Brindisi, notwithstanding its different meter, directly recalls the first of the three *Rigoletto* dances; an offstage banda performs music that is deliberately "indifferent," while onstage the dramatic theme from which the tragedy will unfold is clearly presented (example 2.3).

This stylistic feature will reappear, in a more complex and refined manner, and—because it is placed at the culminating point of the plot—with even more powerful dramatic force, in *Un ballo in maschera*. Once again, the offstage banda performs a tune fairly similar to that of the opening dance in *Rigoletto*; and, perhaps not accidentally, the exposition is again in A♭ major. Here, however, the idea is introduced even before the beginning of the final scene of the opera, during Riccardo's monologue, and serves to characterize by contrast the atmosphere of the forthcoming festivities (example 2.4). The music, yet again deliberately "indifferent," "banal," and "vulgar" (and one could say much about this last adjective),[6] is developed in the next scene, thus fixing through persistent repetition, through its "duration," the basic ambience of the grand party exactly as in *Rigoletto*. Superimposed on this musical background, the conspirators' brief phrases are set in maximum relief (example 2.5).

The entrance of a second orchestra, consisting merely of a small group of strings (as in both *Don Giovanni* and *Rigoletto*), coincides with the last meeting of the lovers Riccardo and Amelia (example 2.6).

This is not the place to offer a close analysis of the subtleties with which Verdi manages to highlight, through a magnificently effective crescendo, the tension between the "indifference" of this impassive little orchestra and the dramatic dialogue that unfolds between the two characters. My main point has been sufficiently stressed: to draw attention to the dramatic and musical richness that is born through this encounter—one far from casual—between Verdi and the Mozart masterpiece.

Postscript

There has of course been much analytical work in this area since the publication of this essay. I should like to mention in particular the critical insights found in Frits Noske, *The Signifier and the Signified—Studies in the Operas of Mozart and Verdi* (The Hague, 1977; reprint, Oxford, 1990); and the new documentary information supplied on *Rigoletto* in Marcello Conati, *La bottega della musica: Verdi e La Fenice* (Milan, 1983).

CHAPTER 2

EXAMPLE 2.1a

MOZART

Example 2.1a, *cont.*

VERDI

Example 2.1b

MOZART

Example 2.1b, *cont.*

MOZART

Example 2.1b, *cont.*

VERDI

Example 2.2

Example 2.3

Example 2.3, *cont.*

Example 2.4

Allegro vivissimo ♩ = 152
parlante
Riccardo
Ah! des-sa è là...
Banda interna
f
R.
po-trei ve-der-la... an-co-ra ri-par-lar-le po-
R.
trei... Ma no: che tut-to or mi strap-pa da lei.

EXAMPLE 2.5

EXAMPLE 2.6

EXAMPLE 2.6, *cont.*

Notes

1. See the postscript to this chapter.

2. An undated fragment of correspondence, quoted by Carlo Gatti in the preface to the facsimile of *L'abbozzo del Rigoletto di Giuseppe Verdi*, edizione fuori commercio a cura del Ministero della Cultura Popolare (Milan, 1941).

3. The complete text is in *I copialettere di Giuseppe Verdi* (Milan, 1913), 109–11.

4. For a more detailed account of this sketch, see chapter 3, pp. 59–70.

5. Abramo Basevi, *Studio sulle opere di Giuseppe Verdi* (Florence, 1859; reprint, Bologna, 1978), 185–86.

6. "La 'volgarità' di Giuseppe Verdi" is the title of the final essay in Alberto Moravia's *L'uomo come fine e altri saggi* (Milan, 1964); this essay is an eloquent example of the hazards encountered when theses are built on conceptual abstractions rather than from the reality of musical sound.

CHAPTER 3

REMARKS ON VERDI'S COMPOSING PROCESS

TO VARYING degrees and in more-or-less obvious ways, Verdi studies have until recently been much influenced—and are in part still influenced—by the manner in which the composer wanted his life and works to be considered. In a certain sense, this "Verdi" personality has determined the directions taken by research on both his art and his life; the image that the composer willed to posterity has unconsciously guided these inquiries, perhaps more tellingly than scholars themselves have been aware. The image of Verdi "the peasant"—devoid of culture, deaf to all that took place around him (especially musical matters), interested merely in his own creations whose principles of organization he drew exclusively from within himself—constitutes a basic cliché that even today enjoys too much currency.[1] A second stereotyped image tells us that Verdi should be considered more a man of the theater than a composer. As a direct consequence Verdi's music is seen as merely "functional" and tends to be understood and judged only in those terms.

However, some of the most recent research is based on a more detailed (and deeper) historical and critical evaluation of already well-known documents; and this—even more than all the new evidence that has emerged—has revealed how these rigid characterizations were in fact encouraged by the composer in order to hide his true self. These new studies have, in short, allowed us to see the fundamental flaws, or at least the incompleteness, of the old picture. But the process of revaluation is far from complete. Even Frank Walker's book,[2] which is the basic starting point for any study of the man Verdi, attempts not to present a new and exhaustively detailed biography but rather to ascertain the accuracy, the extent, and the internal consistency of some of the most widely discussed and controversial moments in the composer's life.

Perhaps the most serious problem caused by superimposing these abstractions onto historical reality occurs in studies that address musical matters: Verdi's operatic language, in light of both its historical context and the basic elements that determine its articulation, has been considered almost entirely in theatrical—or, if one wishes, dramatic—terms. But if it is true that Verdi's work belongs to the musical theater far more than to any other type of musical experience, it is equally the case that the composer expressed himself—realized his ideas—exclusively through musical means; solely through music did he create a theatrical language that is unmistakeably his own. Thus research into Verdi's work must ultimately turn to the musical language considered in its own terms and to the principles that govern its organization. This applies especially to inquiries that attempt to explain his composing process. To elaborate the point: Verdi's dramatic conception takes shape and is realized in its essence through musical means; all writings, all discussion concerned with "dramatic analysis"[3] or, more specifically, with principles of theatrical research,[4] will find greater justification if tested against direct consideration of the musical discourse; such studies will find final and complete confirmation only when they take into consideration the basic elements and tools that the composer used in constructing his musico-dramatic edifice.

Given this situation one can readily appreciate how, although there are several studies of Verdi's composing process that consider the creation of the dramatic skeleton—the collaboration with librettists, the drafting of the literary text on which the score is built—there are hardly any that address musical creation, the composition of the score. A single, important exception is the facsimile edition of the *Rigoletto* sketch, published in 1941:[5] it is the only complete Verdi sketch available at present and is a publication that has given rise to some notable studies.[6] But it is symptomatic of a general trend that even these studies are little more than comparisons between details of the sketch and corresponding passages in the final score and that they are dominated by the idea that the latter improves upon the former (a point that hardly needs to be stressed). No one yet seems to have approached the sketch for what it is, to have considered it as a document that uniquely reveals how Verdi's musical ideas gradually took shape and that allows us to appreciate the process by which those ideas became organized as a complex musico-dramatic structure.

In reality, those who address Verdi's composing process have had to deal with external obstacles: the facts that almost all Verdi's sketches are unavailable for study[7] and that—as with other types of documentary sources on the composer—there is no catalog or even simple list of this type of material.[8] However, the collection that the Istituto di studi verdiani in Parma has for some time been compiling now allows us to approach the problem with a broader and more informed perspective if not with a greater quantity of material.

As with any other artist, a study of Verdi's creative process cannot ignore the historical development of the composer's artistic personality and consequently of his poetics. In fact, this type of inquiry can offer a useful way of testing hypotheses and assertions made on the basis of other factors: a change in the composing process corresponds to an alteration in the general conception of the musical work. Each period of artistic production (probably each single opera) presents individual characteristics that reveal those special problems the composer confronted at that time, with that particular dramatic text—so much so that it is difficult, especially at this preliminary stage, to seek general or absolute principles, valid for each of Verdi's works and for each period of his creative activity. The following study thus offers no more than a detailed consideration of a previously unpublished document (the fragments concerning the finale of *I due Foscari*) and some thoughts on another, already well-known source (the *Rigoletto* sketch). The cautious hypotheses that will emerge are derived from the evidence presented; nothing systematic or definitive is attempted. These are, quite simply, the first results from explorations in almost unknown territory.

First some matters of general significance. There exist complete sketches of Verdi's operas only from *Luisa Miller* (1849) onward;[9] for the operas before *Luisa* we know only of sketches and annotations for separate parts, single scenes, or isolated vocal pieces.[10] As hinted above, this state of affairs is intimately tied to the radical transformation in Verdi's conception of the opera, a change that coincides with his gradual awareness of the necessity—in the years around 1850—to realize in his scores an overall formal unity. Thus distancing himself from the poetics of his Italian operatic predecessors, Verdi no longer conceived of an opera as a sequence of contrasting "situations" isolated from one other, each encapsulated in a dramatic moment (the *situazione*) that characterized it. Each "episode" has a paradigmatic function; it is therefore abstract and thus not necessarily connected to the rest of the action, something that finds its perfect musical equivalent in the closed "number" (aria, duet, chorus, etc.) that revolves around a single key. Verdi instead recognized the need to link the various moments of the dramatic thread, not only by means of contrast (the poetics of contrast between "situations" was already clear to Bellini, for example) but also through a precise articulation of the musical form, resorting when necessary to formal principles derived from instrumental music (notably from the works of the Viennese masters of the period).[11] And thus he gradually moved from sketches of the individual moment, the single situation or scene, to a pre-arranged and clearly articulated laying-out of the entire musical drama.

A second general statement, valid for all documents concerning Verdi's creative musical activity, is that this evidence cannot be evaluated indiscriminately. One cannot, that is, ascribe to all these documents the same significance or the same function, since each refers to a particular phase of this activity, which is usually realized through the definition and the clarification of an initial idea. The term "sketch" does not, then, indicate to which phase of the creative process the document refers; it is at best generic and ambiguous. What is more, there are frequent divergences between the sketch, which we imagine reflects the latest phase of this process of self-clarification, and the final version as we find it in the autograph score (used for the first performance and in the making of the vocal score).[12]

A related problem—one that I do not wish to discuss in detail here—concerns operas like *La traviata* or *Falstaff* in which the final working-out took place long after the first performance. And there are, of course, even more radical attempts at clarification of a first idea: the transformation of *Stiffelio* into *Aroldo*,[13] the journey from the first to the second version of *La forza del destino*, the various revisions to *Don Carlos*. I would suggest, rather, that alterations such as that of *I Lombardi* into *Jérusalem* were in large part prompted by the necessity of adapting an opera born for the Italian stage during the 1840s to the requirements of a different taste, that of the French theater. But I am also aware that these external pressures could—in certain cases, must—have played an important part in some of the operas I mentioned above (for example, in the transformation of *Don Carlos* from a French grand opéra into an Italian *melodramma*); so much so that, in the end, the innumerable problems raised by Verdian revisions intersect only in part with those of the composer's creative process.[14]

THE EARLIEST Verdi sketch I have so far been able to examine is a bifolio of twenty-four-stave music paper in 4° vertical format, housed in the Museum at Busseto (plate 3.1). Identification of the opera to which the fragment belongs, and its exact location in the score, is made easy by the autograph marking that heads fol. 1^r: "Scena ed Aria Doge e Finale ultimo." The text that opens the recitative confirms that we are dealing with *I due Foscari*. Since fol. 1^{r-v} contains only the beginning of the recitative (up to the doge's "mi serbano co[-storo]"), and since fol. 2^{r-v} contains the end of the chorus's exclamation—"[Vedi, abbastanza è misero, ri-]spetta il suo dolor!" and Lucrezia's "O Cielo! già di Foscari s'acclama il successor!"—it is safe to conclude that we have before us the two outermost leaves of a fascicle that contained in its central (lost) section the doge's aria "Questa è dunque l'iniqua mercede" and that the conclusion of the episode (beginning with the doge's Andante "Quel bronzo ferale") must have been on a further fascicle, also missing and probably lost forever. No instruments are indicated, but the layout of the parts and the format of the music paper tell us that this fragment (example 3.1) comes from a fairly advanced stage of composition; however, divergences from the printed score make it clear that we are still some distance from the definitive version.

Apart from the change of key signature (in the definitive version the two-flat signature disappears) and in the orchestral accompaniment's harmonic progression on the first page, the most important alterations occur in the melodic contour of the declamation, as we can see by a comparison of the sketch to the definitive version (example 3.2).

On the second page of the sketch (example 3.3), the most significant modifications again concern the declamation, in this case Lucrezia's outburst. Although the accompanying parts on this second page are probably incomplete, the most important sounding events of the "situation" are clearly notated: in this case the offstage bell that announces to the old doge that his successor has been elected.

Plate 3.1. Verdi, autograph composing score of the "Scena ed Aria Doge e Finale ultimo" from *I due Foscari* (Museo Civico, Busseto), fol. 1^{r}

Plate 3.1, *cont.* Fol. 1[v]

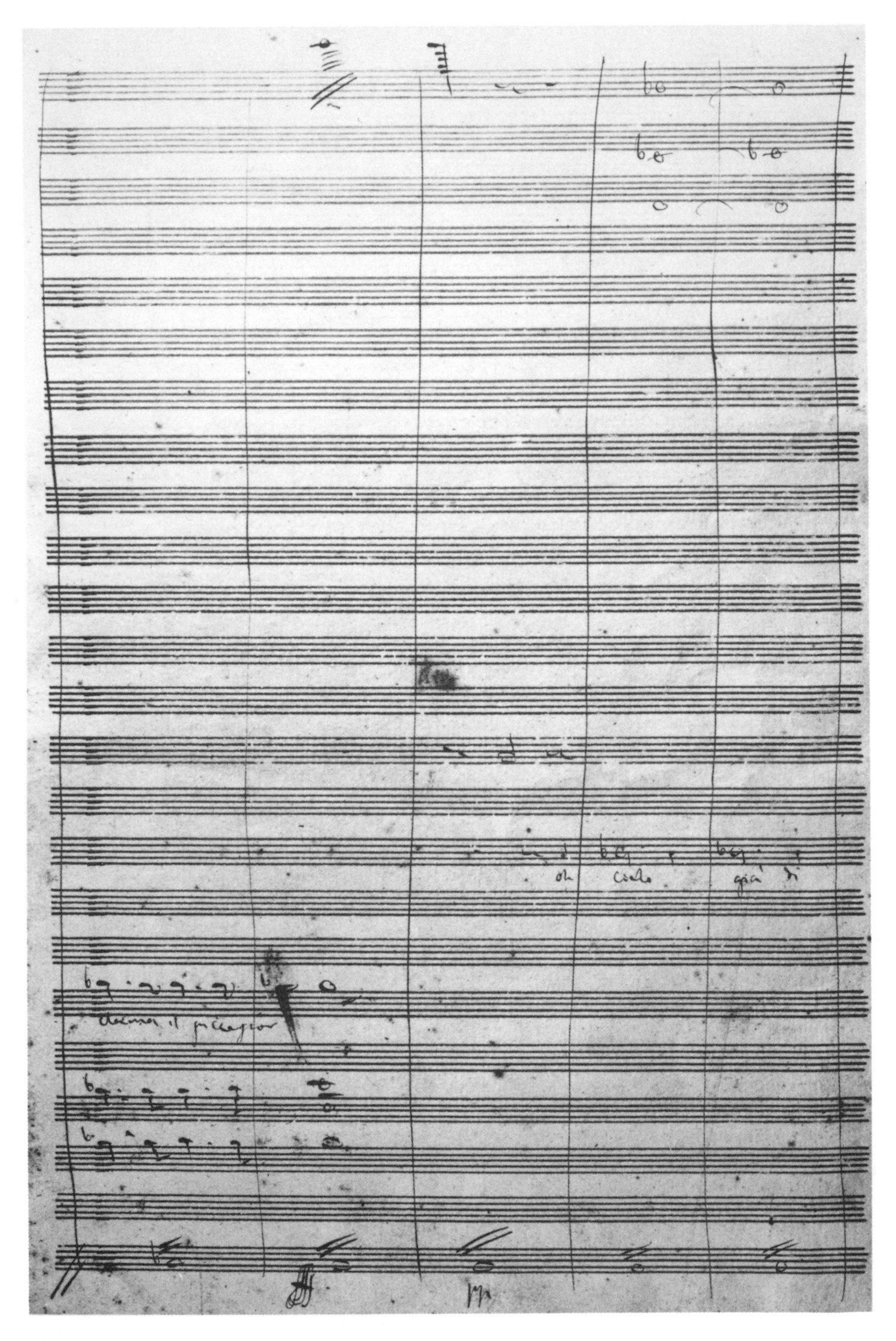

Plate 3.1, *cont.* Fol. 2r

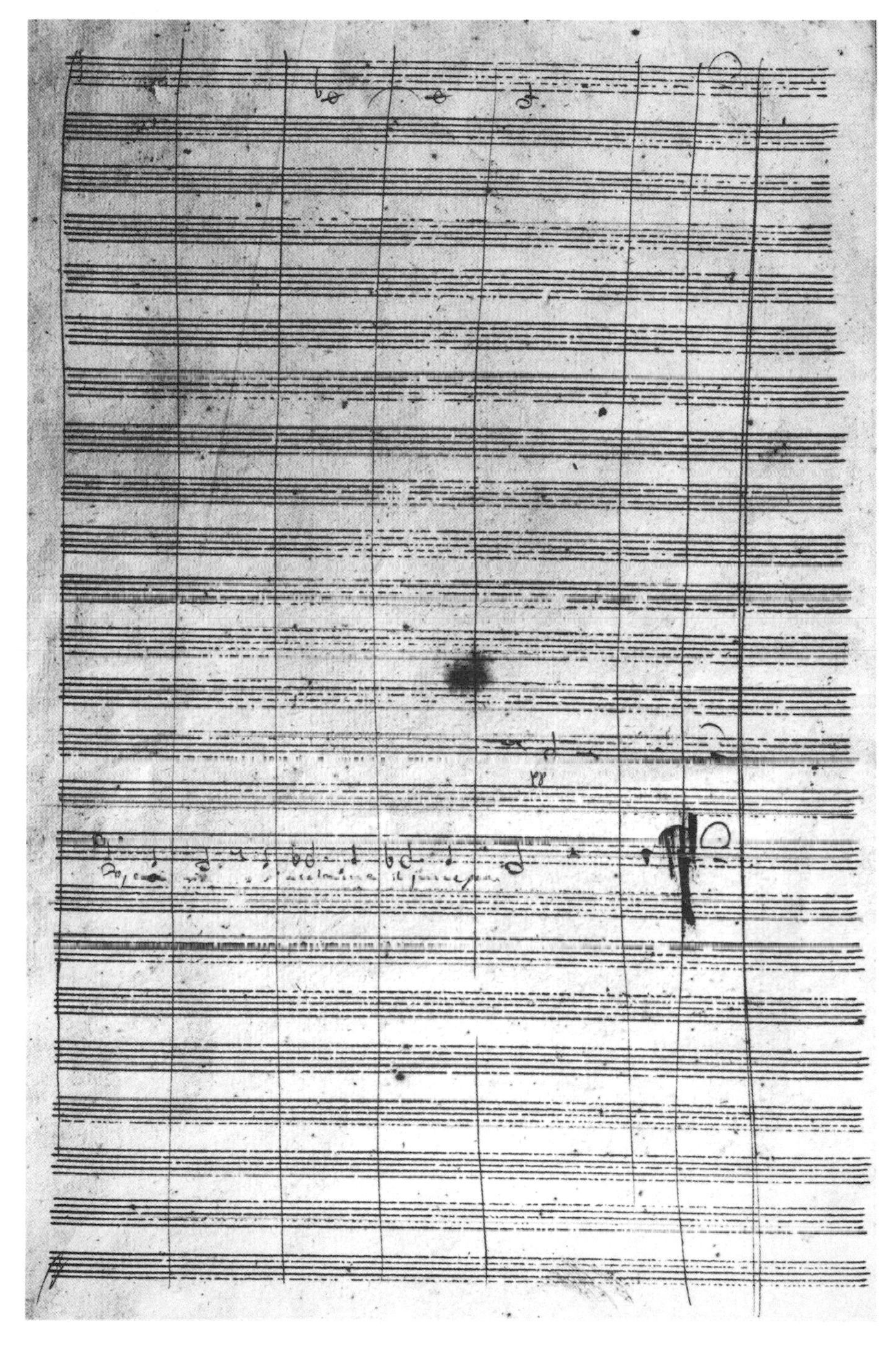

Plate 3.1, *cont.* Fol. 2v

EXAMPLE 3.1

The conclusions one can draw from this early Verdi sketch are extremely limited, both because the fragment is so short and because of the type of music it contains. But at least one point can be made without fear of contradiction: even in this initial phase of his career, Verdi actively felt the need to adapt the melodic gestures of the declamation to a more rigorous musical logic; and this inevitably meant binding them more closely to the dramatic moment. Comparing the two compositional stages, we can see at the opening of the scene how the rhythmic scansion remains almost identical whereas, in the definitive version, the succession of pitches is much changed (at "entrino tosto" the line even takes an opposite direction); if the early declamation is more emphatic, the definitive version moves according to a clear ascending sequence that, starting on A, reaches its peak at the E♭ of "[co-]sto[-ro!]."

In the definitive version of Lucrezia's outburst, the dramatic impact secures maximum force through the repetition of "O Cielo!" and through the upward leap of a fifth from E♭ to high B♭ in the first of the two exclamations; all this was

EXAMPLE 3.1, *cont.*

EXAMPLE 3.2

EXAMPLE 3.3

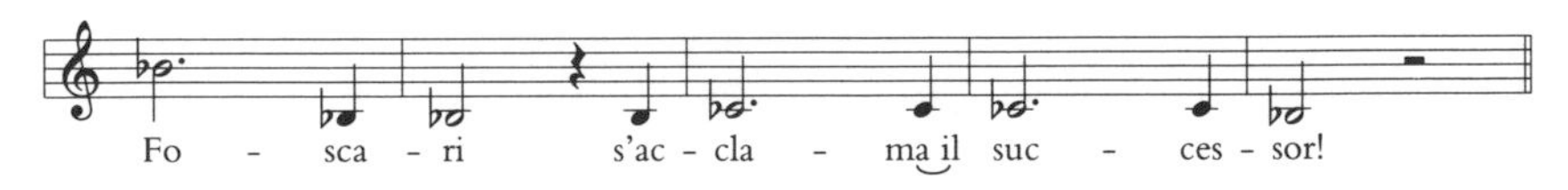

implicit in the sketch version (see, for example, the change in dynamic marking from ***ffff*** to ***pp*** in the bass part at mm. 2–3 of fol. 2ʳ), but in the definitive version the contrast is made fully explicit to the audience.

In comparison with the definitive version, then, the sketch seems to contain *in nuce* the idea that will receive its most precise form at a later stage. In moving from sketch to definitive version Verdi not only gave his musical ideas greater dramatic incisiveness but also expanded and broadened them; in other words, the sketch represents the essence, the nucleus from which the final version will develop. This much seems clear even from such an incomplete fragment as the *I due Foscari* sketch; and the point is fundamental if we are to understand the full significance of sketches for the later operas and, in broader terms, to understand Verdi's creative process.

THE PROBLEM of discovering how Verdi's musical ideas gradually assume their definitive form within a precisely articulated dramatic and musical structure is one that could certainly be clarified by a detailed and thorough study of the *Rigoletto* sketch.[15] As have scholars before me, here I can do no more than examine a few specific problems, to cast a few isolated glimpses into this endlessly fascinating document. I will try above all to discover how some musical ideas take the form we know, leaving aside the other, equally important question of their position and function within the larger dramatic context.

As is already known, the sketch consists of two fascicles that contain a continuous draft of the entire opera. However, for the most part only the melodic line[16] and the bass part are notated. Chords—the vertical structure—are written out only when the harmonies are not "obvious" or when the harmonic progression is in some way significant; indications of orchestration are given only at special moments, when the instrumental timbre takes on an important dramatic function.[17] For all this, one can conclude that at the stage of his career in which Verdi defined in the most precise and exigent form a language that would be unmistakeably his own, melody is still the predominant factor in determining musical style. To analyze certain examples in which (through various phases) the vocal line, or melody, gradually acquires its definitive aspect is thus to inquire into the formation of one of the fundamental elements of Verdi's musical language.

I have chosen from the *Rigoletto* sketch two passages that seem particularly interesting in that we can identify in both three stages through which the musical idea has gradually taken its final shape. The first example reveals Verdi at work on the negative characterization of his protagonist: it is the passage in Act I during which Rigoletto, imitating the duke, replies to the outburst that Monterone unleashes soon after his appearance onstage. In addition to a draft in the main body of the sketch (fol. 5ᵛ, systems 3–6), there is a further version of this section on fol. 1ʳ, in the lower part of the page. Although there is no firm evidence that the version on fol. 5ᵛ is later than that written on the outer leaf, various factors tend to confirm that hypothesis.

If we accept that, at moments in which the sketch version differs from the definitive score, the various creative stages reflect a gradual process of development during which the initial idea grows and takes on greater definition, we must necessarily conclude that the version on the first page of the sketch is earlier than the one on fol. 5ᵛ, given that in the latter we can see a development of the musical discourse, a greater richness of detail, and a closer resemblance to the definitive version. The internal sketch is, then, an intermediate phase between the definitive version and the one that appears on fol. 1ʳ. As examples 3.4a and 3.4b show, we can see in particular a greater differentiation of rhythmic values in the journey from one version to the other.

EXAMPLE 3.4a

Example 3.4b

* First version: D.

Example 3.4b, *cont.*

The opposite idea—that the version on the first page of the sketch is later than the internal one—cannot be supported by convincing evidence. What is more, there are further examples from the *Rigoletto* sketch in which one could reconstruct a similar chronological progression.[18] We can guess that Verdi sometimes stopped in order to work out, "test" on paper, the form of various ideas—ideas that he realized called for greater clarity, for a more exact sense of "belonging" to the scenic situation; and to do this he made use of the outer leaves of the fascicle on which he was then working.

But the problem Verdi had to confront was not simply how to achieve a more convincing declamation. For we have here a very special type of recitative: a character (Rigoletto), speaking as if he were another (the duke), reveals to those onstage and to the audience the depths to which he has fallen, so much so that he eventually brings down on himself Monterone's curse, the curse around which the drama hinges. Verdi thus had to emphasize two aspects. The first was that of caricature: Rigoletto's discourse is the parody of a solemn speech. Verdi gradually achieved this, as witnessed through his compositional drafts, by increasing the contrast between durational values; see, for example, "Voi congiuraste," in which the simple enunciation of the first version becomes ever more emphatic in the second and the final versions: on the syllable "[congiu-] ra[-ste]" there is a quarter-note in the first version, a whole note in the second, and two whole notes plus a quarter in the final score.

Verdi's second task was to underline Rigoletto's "anima nera" (black soul) by making the best use of the most obvious musical sign of negative characterization: the unison.[19] In the first version its use can be seen—albeit not explicitly notated—in the orchestral interjections between the baritone's phrases (this is confirmed by looking at the second version of the passage); the unison here is veiled, it carries no powerful characterizing force. With the second version the composer felt the need to identify Rigoletto with this musical device even before he spoke, and so he added four measures of orchestral introduction. In the final version this becomes six measures, all unison, in which Verdi used rhythmic figures  taken from the orchestral interjections separating the protagonist's first two phrases, an idea that figured in the first version but was then rejected. In the score this passage evolved into a sibilant figure (example 3.5) repeated an octave and then two octaves lower, just as in the sketch the simple leap of an octave was repeated. We might also notice, again in connection with the unison as an element of negative characterization, the transformation from the second to the definitive version of the orchestral part that accompanies the syllables "[congiu-]ra[-ste]" and "noi": a figure in parallel thirds is altered to one in unison or octaves (with an intervallic progression that echoes in inversion that of mm. 4–6 of the orchestral introduction). The cell quoted below (example 3.6)—which disappeared in the final version—must also have been an element of negative characterization (again the leap of an octave!). This figure, however, is almost identical to the pedal point that Verdi first sketched for the introduction to the Rigoletto-Sparafucile dialogue (again in Act I) and that he preserved only at the center of that dialogue. There is no better illustration of the attention the composer gave—even at a very early stage of the composing process—to elements that would serve to connect and unify the various musical sections of the score.

Example 3.5

Example 3.6

The melody entrusted in the definitive version to a solo violoncello and double bass (muted and in octaves), and which accompanies the dialogue between Rigoletto and Sparafucile (alias Saltabadil), is a different case. An early version (my reason for this dating is the same as that advanced in connection with the Rigoletto recitative) is again found on fol. 1ʳ of the sketch's first fascicle (plate 3.2), in the center of the page; a second version, which differs from the final reading both in melodic shape and in its relation to the vocal parts, appears on fol. 6ᵛ (plate 3.3). This example is a different case from the one discussed above, first because Verdi's basic problem here was not tied to word declamation: here, the instrumental melody serves as the pivot for the entire duet, which is constructed according to a pattern that we might define in broad terms as variation form. Its various sections have a structure (and duration) that was fixed by the time Verdi wrote the main body of the sketch: note especially the central section of the duet, beginning with "E quanto spendere" and ending with the exclamation "(Demonio!)," which is worked out in every detail. Since the structural weight is clearly entrusted to the orchestral part (it is there, and not in the vocal part, that the variation form is articulated), Verdi had to find a melody that could characterize the situation and at the same time undergo musical development independently of the accompanying text. It is in this sense highly indicative of Verdi's larger formal concerns that he searched first for the contour, the melodic shape, independent of both its orchestral accompaniment and the vocal parts. On the first page of the sketch fascicle the melody appears as shown in example 3.7; example 3.8 reveals how it is developed in the main body of the sketch.

In the second version the melody has *almost* reached its definitive form; even the vertical relationships, the harmony, are near their final shape. However, its relationship with the vocal parts is still far from settled. A comparative analysis of the first and second versions shows that Verdi's central problem was to find the precise form of the melody. From the beginning the basic phrase structure, though not yet fully defined, is a clear 4 + 4 + 8. He thus needed to elaborate the melodic contour within this larger form, to work on the interval structure in relation to the phrase's overall development, in order to give the melody both maximum flexibility and maximum definition of character. We see immediately that the alterations occur for the most part on the upbeats of the measure (the eighth-notes), whereas pitches on the beat (the dotted quarter-notes) almost always remain unchanged. In the opening eight measures of the first version, all the strong beats preceded by a lower note are separated by a third from that note, hence the monotony and rigidity of melodic movement (parallel to the rhythmic uniformity) that continues in the final three measures, where the strong beats are always preceded by the note a semitone lower. As mentioned earlier, the melody reaches what is almost its definitive shape in the second version; the second and sixth measures are a minor exception: Verdi's desire to eliminate the rigid symmetry of ascending thirds led him to experiment with a rather unfortunate E or F (the note is difficult to read), later altered to the definitve reading.

Plate 3.2. Initial sketch for the melody of the Act I Rigoletto-Sparafucile duet, *Rigoletto* sketch, fol. 1r

Plate 3.3. *Rigoletto* sketch, fol. 6ᵛ

EXAMPLE 3.7

EXAMPLE 3.8
Quel vec - chio ma - le - di - va - mi
First version:
va
va non ho nien - te
First version:
Si - gnor
Si - gnor
né il

EXAMPLE 3.8, *cont.*

The addition of the vertical dimension—the instrumental bass—causes interesting changes in mm. 9–11 of the early fol. 1^{r} version. The caesura (accompanied by a more precise, definite sense of cadential closure, F–A–F instead of F–E–F) makes the end of the first part of the melody (i.e., the first eight measures) clearer. More important, however, it clarifies the bow shape of the eight measures that follow: in the first version the ascending movement of the line is powerfully interrupted by the descending movement of m. 10 and by the bow form of mm. 11 and 12 (C–D♭–E♭–F–E♭).

The main interest in the comparison between the second and definitive versions lies, however, in the new relationship established between the vocal and orchestral parts.[20] Having developed the four-measure introduction into ten measures (an alteration whose harmonic implications would bear some scrutiny), Verdi began an early version of the dialogue between Sparafucile and Rigoletto at the end of the second measure of the orchestral melody—in an even earlier stage, halfway through that same measure.[21] In this version, the voices move in unison with (or at least are very closely tied to) the orchestral melody, always observing the strong beats. The graphic layout of the sketch, and certain incongruities that would result from the vertical combination of the parts, make clear that Verdi first worked out the instrumental part, then added the voices. In this intermediate phase, the vocal parts duplicate (though they do not literally repeat) the orchestral melody. But Verdi wanted the instrumental melody to be entirely self-sufficient and the voices onstage to move independently; he intended, that is, to realize the passage contrapuntally, and so he arrived at the idea of a superimposition of highly individual melodic lines. The imposing musical richness of the passage arises directly from this extraordinary intuition. In order to highlight sufficiently the instrumental melody, Verdi "reduced" the vocal lines; he began the dialogue only when the exposition of the first part of the melody was completed: the first four measures of the cello and double bass line thus dominate the situation; the relationship between the instruments and the voices is perfectly defined. At the same time, Verdi shortened and further differentiated the durational values of the notes in the vocal line, ♪♪ ⟶ ♪. ♬, so making the declamation of the passage more lively, more forward-moving and, above all, more individual. This type of declamation is preserved throughout the dialogue. My reference to the "vocal line" is deliberate: the two voices alternate but are never superimposed or musically differentiated. Verdi conceived the two parts as a single melodic unity, separate from and in contrast to the line entrusted to the two solo strings.

One last example from the *Rigoletto* sketch: the orchestral measures that begin the final act, introducing the recitative between Rigoletto and Gilda (fascicle 2, fol. 4^{v}, first and second systems). The sketch version differs so greatly from the final score that some have considered them two different ideas;[22] however, a closer look makes clear that we are dealing with the same basic material, transformed—with impressive logical coherence—from an accumulation of vertical sonorities to a polyphonic texture.[23] In the sketch this brief introduction appears as shown in example 3.9.

EXAMPLE 3.9

The phrase grouping of 3 + 3 + 5 is obvious: the second group, although slightly varied at the beginning, essentially repeats the first. In the first six measures the melodic movement lies in a low register, circling around an E pedal. In the five measures that follow only a middle-register voice is notated; this takes up the melodic movement started by the low voice and moves in the opposite (i.e., ascending) direction; it concludes, descending by step, on the E of the beginning. Basically we have a monodic prolongation of E: the note Verdi felt characterized the entire situation. In the final version the composer lengthened the first phrase by a measure, eliminated the almost literal repetition, and prolonged the melodic phrase. But, most important, he took away the descending bass figure that connects the octave E–E and introduced in melodic form what the sketch presented simultaneously: the octave, originally at the beginning of the sketch, is now at the end of the phrase. The E now appears only in the third measure, and the phrase begins with a single melodic line—one that, however, suggests linearly the two (and then three) voices introduced simultaneously in the third measure (example 3.10).

EXAMPLE 3.10

A fourth voice appears in this third measure: the melodic gesture in the upper voice (not fortuitously, an almost literal inversion of the melodic movement of the first measure) divides into two. The second four-measure phrase is nearer to the sketch: it too is lengthened by two measures, but again the monodic movement is broadened into a coherent polyphonic complex. Once the first part's descending melodic movement in the low register was eliminated, it was natural that its ascending reply also disappeared; instead the descending stepwise phrase that in the sketch extended only to a fifth is stretched to an octave and transferred to the bass, and it is to this bass gesture that the polyphonic weave of the other three parts then adapts.

CLEARLY, no definitive statements about Verdi's creative process can emerge from our discussion of these few examples. First, we have merely considered a few cases in which the final draft and the preceding versions differ notably; in many other places (only a note-by-note comparison could say precisely how many) the sketch and final version coincide fairly exactly. Second, we have been examining examples taken from operas of the composer's youth and early maturity. So long as the sketches for the other operas remain unavailable to scholars, we cannot state that Verdi had a single way of musically conceiving an operatic score; nor can we know whether the procedure may vary according to the dramatic structure he is setting to music. Such chronological and quantitative limitations make any conclusion risky and arbitrary. However, and bearing in mind these limitations, it nevertheless seems legitimate to affirm that when a sketch differs (even drastically) from its corresponding passage in the final version, we are not in most cases seeing an initial idea that was later abandoned and replaced by another. We have, rather, a first formulation of that idea, one that the composer himself seems not yet to have precisely worked out but that he wrote down in order to elaborate it and give it a greater sense of "pertinence," until it reached the musical shape corresponding exactly to his intentions, thus adjusting it to the overall conception of the opera.

Postscript

Since the publication of this essay (in 1971), three important bibliographical items have been published:

1. Cecil Hopkinson, *A Bibliography of the Works of Giuseppe Verdi, 1813–1901*, vols. 1 (New York, 1973), containing the vocal and instrumental works and excluding the operas, and 2 (New York, 1978), containing the operas. This work is primarily devoted to the printed sources and identifies their chronology and relationships.
2. Martin Chusid, *A Catalog of Verdi's Operas*, Music Indexes and Bibliographies no. 5 (Hackensack, N.J., 1974), which lists autographs, manu-

scripts, and printed sources, as well as printed librettos, of all Verdi's operas. As Chusid says on p. 1, "This catalog [. . .] seeks to answer two questions about Verdi resources: what they contain and where they may be found."

3. Maria Adelaide Bacherini Bartoli, "Aggiunte integrazioni e rettifiche alla *Bibliography of the Works of Giuseppe Verdi* di Cecil Hopkinson. Edizioni verdiane nella Biblioteca Nazionale Centrale di Firenze," *Studi verdiani* 4 (1986–87): 110–35.

Concerning the problem of sources for the composing process earlier than the sketches as described by Carlo Gatti, recent studies by Philip Gossett and others suggest that Verdi made such sketches at least from the time of *Nabucco*; see Philip Gossett, "The Composition of *Ernani*," in Carolyn Abbate and Roger Parker, eds., *Analyzing Opera: Verdi and Wagner* (Berkeley and Los Angeles, 1989), 27–55; also published and partially modified in *Ernani Yesterday and Today*, in *Verdi* (Bollettino dell'Istituto nazionale di studi verdiani) 10 (Parma, 1989), 65–95.

On the relationship between *Stiffelio* and *Aroldo*, see Vito Levi, "*Stiffelio* e il suo rifacimento (*Aroldo*)," *Atti del I° congresso internazionale di studi verdiani* (Parma, 1969), 172–75; and see Renzo Bragantini, "Da *Stiffelio* ad *Aroldo*: la storia come censura"; Julian Budden, "Differences in the Musical Language between *Stiffelio* and *Aroldo*"; and Martin Chusid, "Apropos *Aroldo*, *Stiffelio*, and *Le pasteur*, with a Short List of Nineteenth-Century Performances of *Aroldo*," in *Tornando a Stiffelio. Popolarità, rifacimento, messinscena, effettismo e altre "cure" nella drammaturgia del Verdi romantico*, ed. Giovanni Morelli, 89–96, 273–80, and 280–303 (Florence, 1987).

I would be hesitant to maintain today, as I did in 1971, that the transformation of *Stiffelio* into *Aroldo* is simply an "attempt at clarification."

Notes

1. Naturally this opinion has been "constructed" through the few biographical documents that Verdi allowed to be disseminated—for example, the appendix to chapter 6 of Arthur Pougin, *Giuseppe Verdi—Vita aneddotica . . . con note ed aggiunte di Folchetto* (Milan, 1881), 39–46. "Folchetto" would have us believe that Verdi was completely unaware of the publication of the appendix, while in fact we know that the composer even read proofs (see Frank Walker, *The Man Verdi* [London, 1962; reprint, Chicago, 1982], 3). Also of interest is the chapter dedicated to Verdi in Michele Lessona, *Volere è potere* (Florence, 1869), 287–307. For an estimate of the different values of these narratives with reference to one specific episode, see chapter 1, pp. 9–12. But the composer's rich musical culture, especially his concern with contemporary developments, can be seen from countless direct and indirect remarks in his correspondence with close collaborators and trusted friends.

2. See n. 1.

3. Typical examples of this method of considering Verdi's works might be Andrea Della Corte, *Le sei più belle opere di Giuseppe Verdi* (Milan, 1957); and Massimo Mila, *Giuseppe Verdi*, 2d ed. (Bari, 1958); there are also more recent books by non-Italian authors, such as Charles Osborne, *The Complete Operas of Verdi* (London, 1969).

4. The most recent is Leo Karl Gerhartz, *Die Auseinandersetzungen des jungen Giuseppe Verdi mit dem Literarischen Drama—Ein Beitrag zur szenischen Strukturbestimmung der Oper* (Berlin, 1968), which is particularly valuable for its cultural perspectives.

5. *L'abbozzo del Rigoletto di Giuseppe Verdi*, edizione fuori commercio a cura del Ministero della Cultura Popolare (Milan, 1941).

6. See especially Gino Roncaglia, "L'*abbozzo* del Rigoletto," in *Galleria verdiana (studi e figure)* (Milan, 1959), 87–100; and Ildebrando Pizzetti, "Insegnamenti del Rigoletto," in *Verdi e La Fenice* (Venice, 1951), 68–72.

7. Some pages from these sketches are reproduced (though they are not easily legible) in Carlo Gatti, *Verdi nelle immagini* (Milan, 1941), 64–65 (*La traviata*), 184 (*Un ballo in maschera*), 186 (*Il trovatore* and *Aida*), and 187 (*Falstaff* and *Otello*).

8. See the postscript to the present chapter.

9. Carlo Gatti, who was allowed to examine the originals, states this in the introduction to the facsimile of the *Rigoletto* sketch cited in n. 5.

10. See the postscript to the present chapter.

11. On this topic, there are some interesting comments from Ernö Lendvai, "Verdi's Formgeheimnisse," in *Atti del I° congresso internazionale di studi verdiani* (Parma, 1969), 157–71, even though I would stress that studies based on this kind of approach should be concerned more with general structural principles than with correspondences between minute lexical details. For another type of approach, also published in the volume of *Atti* cited here, see János Kovács, "Zum Spätstil Verdis," 132–44, especially 134–37.

12. See the postscript to the present chapter.

13. See the postscript to the present chapter.

14. On this topic, see Wolfgang Osthoff's seminal study "Die beiden Boccanegra-Fassungen und der Beginn von Verdis Spätwerk," *Analecta musicologica* 1 (1963): 70–89.

15. See the postscript to the present chapter.

16. Or melodic lines, when there is an ensemble; the Act IV quartet (fascicle 2, fols. 5^v–6^r) is particularly remarkable.

17. It is interesting to note the clarity with which Verdi "hears" the instrumental timbre at the beginning of the storm in Act IV (fascicle 2, fol. 6^v, fourth system): in the Allegro that begins the "Recitativo senza le appoggiature," a call for "oboe" is made next to the high A, whereas immediately afterward, next to the D–A fifth in the bass, we read "Violoncello."

18. In addition to those passages examined here, one finds other examples in the *Rigoletto* sketch, on fol. 1^r: a melody in A major, not used later—or at least transformed out of all recognition—and a first version of the melody that accompanies the Rigoletto-Sparafucile duet (see below); on fol. 1^v occur what seem to me four different attempts to define the duke's melody in the concertato that concludes the opening scene of the opera (it is difficult to accept the identification proposed by Roncaglia [see n. 6], 88); on the verso of the last folio of fascicle 2 occurs a first version of the "La donna è mobile" melody (on the relationship of this to the definitive version, see Luigi Dallapiccola, "Words and

Music in Italian Nineteenth-Century Opera" [see chapter 1, n. 31] esp. 203–4); and two initial versions of the Rigoletto-Gilda duet at the close of Act IV.

19. For a definition of this important aspect of Verdian poetics, and for numerous clarifying examples, see Péter Pál Várnai, "Contributi per uno studio della tipizzazione negativa nelle opere verdiane—Personaggi e situazioni," in *Atti del I° congresso* (see n. 11), 268–75, esp. 269 and 274.

20. Some interesting remarks on this section of the sketch are offered by Roncaglia (see n. 6), 93–94, and especially by Pizzetti (see n. 6), 67–70, in connection with the melodic and rhythmic changes to "Quel vecchio maledivami!"

21. This last point is proved by the rests and by the two notes, F–A, later canceled.

22. See Roncaglia, 98.

23. An analogous process—of the horizontal development of an initially vertical idea—is discussed by Roger Sessions (with reference to his own music) in *The Musical Experience of the Composer, the Performer, and the Listener* (Princeton, 1959), 52–53.

CHAPTER 4

THOUGHTS FOR *ALZIRA*

THE COMPOSITIONAL process—the activity through which a composer organizes and develops his musical ideas in order to reach the definitive form of a work of art—is closely connected to the artist's poetics; or, more precisely, it is a direct consequence and manifestation of it. The remark is so elementary as to seem almost banal; but it is worth repeating, if for no other reason than because the document at the center of this chapter reinforces its validity with extraordinary clarity. Moreover, the equation between compositional process and realization of the poetics allows for an important verification, one otherwise difficult to achieve: to establish with a certain degree of precision the moment, the period in which this poetics asserted itself, or at least to locate its first manifestations.

It is now commonly accepted that the fundamental characteristic of Verdi's poetics is that of realizing a musico-dramatic unity in the context of an entire score—more specifically, to obtain this unity through a complex, articulated system of "signs" valid through the unfolding of the entire dramatic action.[1] The most striking testimony to this unitary conception—a conception that, it must be stressed, was revolutionary within the Italian operatic tradition—lies in those documents that bear witness to the compositional process, the sketches that chart the unfolding of an entire score, reduced to systems of two or at most three staves on which are indicated (on the uppermost staff) the vocal part—or parts if we are dealing with an ensemble piece—and (on the lowest staff) the bass line. We know that these sketches exist for all the Verdi operas from *Luisa Miller* onward, and scholars have long been able to refer to a facsimile of the *Rigoletto* sketch, a source that was a constant help in establishing the composer's intentions to those engaged in the critical edition of that opera.[2] I have discussed elsewhere in this book (see chapter 3) the word "sketch" as a description of these extraordinary documents (and have remarked that the term is too generic to illustrate their true nature and importance); I have also dealt with some pages that illustrate Verdi's creative activity during the making of his artistic personality: an autograph fragment from the score of *I due Foscari*, which contains a sketch of that opera's third-act finale.[3] I remarked there how the rejected pages from the autograph of *I due Foscari* have at least one point in common with the later *Rigoletto* sketch: they prove, beyond any doubt, that progress from an initial to a definitive phase is not the result of a haphazard or confused trying-out of various musical ideas; it concerns, rather, the establishing, in the definitive version, of the exact temporal dimension of the dramatic-musical event: a perfectly controlled measuring of its durations and, at the same time, a precise, functional definition in musical terms of the entire scene, brought about through the elimination of superfluous melodic gestures.[4]

The document that forms the basis of this chapter bears witness to a further aspect often revealed in the *Rigoletto* sketch: the need, within the terms of Verdi's poetics, to create a continuity in the unfolding of the dramatic discourse, to conceive it as an uninterrupted flow of events that are all equally functional, so that the closed forms and the connecting tissue of recitative constitute an organic whole *even at the moment of their original conception*. It is for this reason that I have thought it appropriate to give the sketches of entire operas a name borrowed from Beethoven studies and thus call them "continuity drafts."

THE LIBRARY of the Gesellschaft der Musikfreunde in Vienna is justly famous for its collection of autograph manuscripts by Beethoven, Haydn, Schubert, and Brahms; but, so far as I am aware, no one has yet discussed the Verdi autograph housed there.[5] It is a sketch consisting of a page of manuscript paper containing twenty-four staves in upright format,[6] notated in Verdi's hand on both sides. On the side I shall call the recto there are eight systems of three staves each. On the verso there are again eight systems: the first six contain only two staves, whereas the last two again contain three staves (see plates 4.1 and 4.2).

The text at the start of the recto allows for easy identification of the sketch. It contains the chorus that ends the Prologue of *Alzira*, "Dio della guerra, i tuoi furori," the exultant song of the Incas precipitated by Zamoro's announcement that their compatriots are ready to rise up against the violence of the Spanish invaders. The piece turns out to be a dialogue between the choral masses and Zamoro, the "coryphaeus," entirely built on the rhythmic cell shown in example 4.1, or on the cell's second half. Example 4.2 gives the passage as it appears in modern vocal scores.[7]

EXAMPLE 4.1

On the recto of the folio now in Vienna (probably written in Naples during the summer of 1845, given that the premiere of *Alzira* took place there on 12 August of that year[8]) we find the forty-five measures that comprise this final chorus of the Prologue, before the stretta at "Poco più animato."

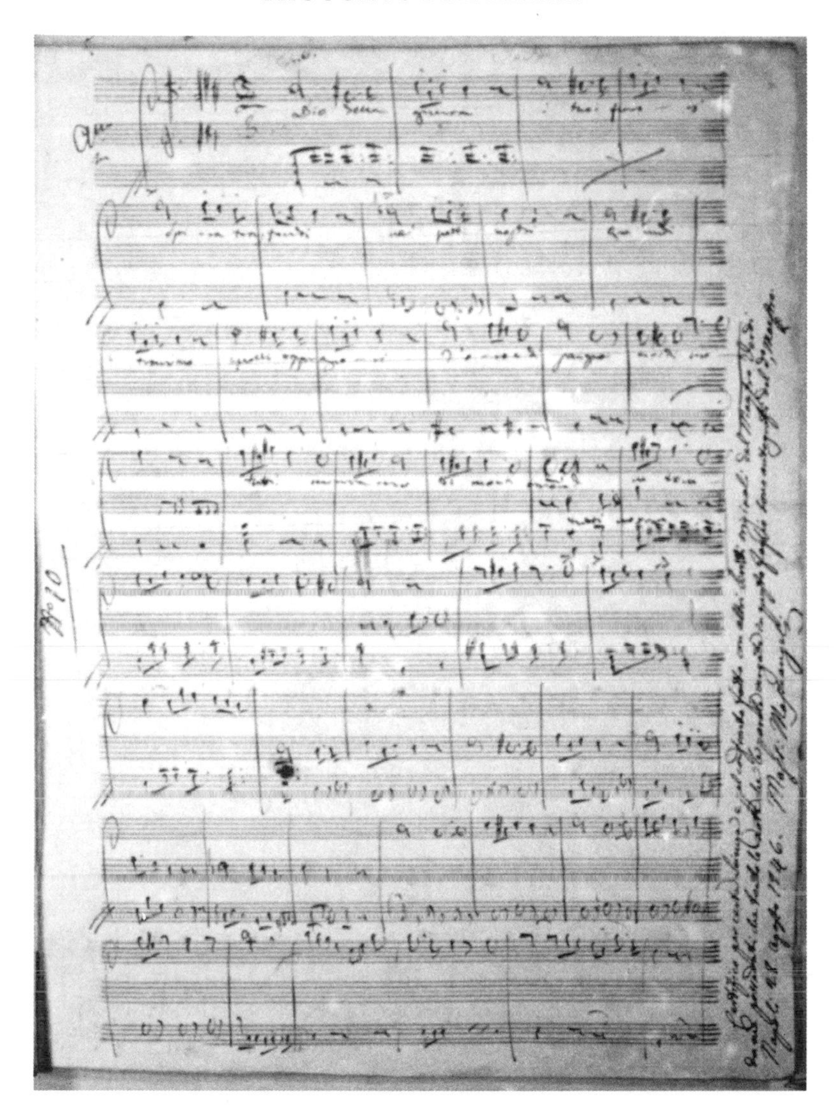

Plate 4.1. Sketch for the conclusion of the Prologue in *Alzira* (Library of the Gesellschaft der Musikfreunde, Vienna, Ms. IV.66875), recto of the folio

Plate 4.2. Verso of the same folio

Example 4.2

Allegro moderato grandioso
tutta forza
Zamoro
Dio del - la guer - ra, i tuoi fu-
Coro
Dio del - la guer - ra, i tuoi fu-
Dio del - la guer - ra, i tuoi fu-
tutta forza
Z.
ro - ri spi - ra, tra - sfon - di
ro - ri spi - ra, tra - sfon - di
ro - ri spi - ra, tra - sfon - di

EXAMPLE 4.2, *cont.*

Example 4.2, *cont.*

EXAMPLE 4.2, *cont.*

EXAMPLE 4.2, *cont.*

Example 4.2, *cont.*

EXAMPLE 4.2, *cont.*

The differences between this and the definitive version are very slight, involving only a few secondary rhythmic and melodic details; the duration of the two versions is identical. What, then, was the problem that Verdi wished to resolve when he set about drafting this sketch? A comparison with the printed libretto for the first performance of the opera is, in this respect, revealing. For the conclusion of the Prologue, Cammarano had created (and then printed in the libretto) a simple Incas' chorus, without Zamoro's participation.[9] The idea of alternating the music of the "Americani" with that of their young hero was, then, entirely Verdi's, and it took concrete shape at the moment when the composer set to work on our sketch, with the aim of determining the formal articulation of this idea and its "texture."

We might consider the layout of the sketch at the top of the page. It is clear that two staves per system were insufficient, and the initial brace after the tempo indication ("All[egro] m[oderato]") unequivocally stretches through three. On the highest of these Verdi wrote a tenor clef, a key signature of three sharps, and a time signature of 3/4; on the staff below he wrote a treble clef (N.B.!), the three-sharp signature, and a single numeral 3 (part of 3/4) as time signature; there is no clef, key signature, or time signature on the lowest staff, but the harmonic foundation is clearly established by an A in the bass and by the repeated eighth-note triplets that complete the tonic chord, explicitly indicated in the first two measures and continued (by a repeat sign) for two more measures.

Having established the linear movement of the piece and its harmonic foundation, Verdi felt with increasing urgency the need to articulate this very simple melodic design (recall that we are dealing with a hymn of exultation sung by "good savages") with contrasting material, placed at the most important structural points so that the entire piece achieved maximum definition of character. But he did not yet know *how* to achieve this result. First he thought of the orchestra: in the sixteenth measure—the end of the first quatrain, a point additionally marked by a large fermata in the bass staff of the preceding measure—he placed on the second staff an interjection, an E repeated on the following rhythm:  .[10] In the definitive version this idea was given to the winds, with a slightly different rhythmic figure:  . But four measures later, again on the second staff and with no indication of a change of clef or key signature, we have a first (if still embryonic) choral intervention, sung to the words "tutti morran"—an intervention that will be developed in the definitive version into three-part chords and that must be read in tenor clef (i.e., not in treble clef, as was the preceding orchestral fragment). It is clear that the voice on the uppermost staff is now no longer that of the "Tutti," as indicated at the beginning of the sketch, but rather that of the "coryphaeus" Zamoro, whose soloistic intervention in the definitive version will begin when he takes up the third line of what Cammarano had conceived as a chorus.[11] The choral interjection that occurs three bars later (to the same words, one assumes, since this time they are not written out), has a function—and text—analogous to this first intervention, as we can see from its development in the definitive version. By means of a modulatory section[12] (made more effective by contrast with the otherwise simple style of the piece), we return at the end of the sixth line to the tonic, A, in time to give the chorus (on the second staff) a reprise of the original phrase.

From now on Verdi had very clear ideas: once the chorus has completed the exposition of the last two lines with a progression from tonic to dominant, Zamoro alone concludes by repeating these two lines, which are in their turn punctuated in the definitive version with cries of "Morran" from the unison chorus.

The layout of the poetic text, first as it appears in Cammarano's libretto, then in the Vienna sketch, and finally in the definitive version (see table 4.1), neatly illustrates the gradual but definite transformation that Verdi effected.[13] The two quatrains of *quinario doppio* imagined by Cammarano are, as it were, split at the center by Zamoro's interventions; the latter sum up and synthesize his compatriots' feelings of revenge, creating a dynamically more articulated and thus more effective dimension to the scene.

CAMMARANO - Libretto	VERDI - Sketch	VERDI - Score
TUTTI Nume dell'armi, i tuoi furori Spira, trasfondi ne' petti nostri.	TUTTI Dio della guerra i tuoi furori Spira trasfondi ne' petti nostri	TUTTI Dio della guerra, i tuoi furori spira, trasfondi ne' petti nostri.
Quei crudi tremino, quegli oppressori D'oro, e di sangue avidi mostri!	Que crudi tremino quelli oppressori d'oro e di sangue avidi mo-[stri!]	ZAMORO Que' crudi tremino, quegli oppressori! d'oro e di sangue avidi mostri!
Tutti morranno di morti orrende,	tutti morranno di morti orrend[e,]	tutti morranno di morti orrende,
	[CORO] tutti morran	CORO tutti tutti morran
Nè tomba un solo, nè rogo avrà!	[ZAMORO] ne tom-[ba un solo, nè rogo avrà!	ZAMORO tutti morranno di morti orrende,
	CORO tutti morran	CORO tutti tutti morran.
	ZAMORO nè tomba un solo, nè rogo, nè rogo avrà!	ZAMORO nè tomba un solo, nè rogo, nè rogo avrà!
L'odio, che atroce il cor n'accende, De' lor cadaveri si pascerà!	CORO L'odio che atroce il cor ne accende, de' lor cadaveri si pascerà!	CORO L'odio che atroce il cor ne accende, de' lor cadaveri si pascerà!
	ZAMORO L'odio che atroce il cor ne accende, de' lor cadaveri, de' lor cadaveri / si pascerà!]	ZAMORO L'odio che atroce
		CORO Morran.
		ZAMORO il cor ne accende
		CORO Morran.
		ZAMORO de' lor cadaveri, de' lor cadaveri / si pascerà!

Table 4.1. Poetic text of the conclusion of the Prologue of *Alzira*, as shown in Cammarano's printed libretto, Verdi's Vienna sketch, and the final version

The verso of the Vienna sketch begins, as mentioned earlier, with a decisive change: we move from three-staff to two-staff systems. At the moment in which he proceeded to create the stretta section, Verdi grasped that to give it full significance as a closing unit he had to eliminate the contrast, the dialogue of the preceding measures, and reunite his vocal forces. The rhythmic pulse of the stretta is clear from the beginning; it is characterized by a strong sense of syncopation, created through placing a relatively long note on the two "weak" beats of the 3/4 measure.

At first Verdi imagined the rhythmic shape of the stretta, a pattern that echoes on its first beat the eighth-note triplets of the preceding chorus, as follows: [3] ♪♪♪ 𝅗𝅥 | ♪♪♪ 𝅗𝅥 | But after seven measures, and probably while he was writing the sixth and seventh measures at the end of the first system (in which one sees the pattern ♩ 𝅗𝅥 | ♩ 𝅗𝅥 |), Verdi realized that by repeating that rhythmic idea the differentiation between the chorus and its stretta was weakened: he needed instead to develop a figure that would emphasize the strong beat of the measure. Starting the draft of the stretta afresh on the second system, he decided on the syncopated pattern of the final two measures of the first system and accentuated it further by transforming the first note from a quarter to an eighth-note (preceded by a rest he omitted to write), a pattern that in the definitive version will even become: 𝄾. 𝅘𝅥𝅯 𝅗𝅥 | 𝄾. 𝅘𝅥𝅯 𝅗𝅥 |.[14] What is more, he added on the second staff—which had remained empty in the preceding system—another voice (in bass clef!) that, after repeating in unison the first two notes of the upper voice, then moves in counterpoint against it, creating that contrasting pattern of strong beats that he had felt to be so essential.

To understand what occurs in the subsequent measures, it will be helpful to consider first the definitive version of the entire stretta (see example 4.3), paying particular attention to its formal articulation:

section:	A	A	B	B	C	C	C
measures:	4	4	2	2	1	1	1 + 10 closing

The stretta consists, then, of three distinct rhythmic-melodic figures of progressively shorter duration, each of which is repeated (in the case of figure C, repeated twice). This complex articulation became clear to Verdi while he was drafting our sketch. Figure A was defined in the first four measures of the second system; for its reiteration the composer needed only to indicate the incipit and the duration, thus leaving empty its third and fourth measures. Figure B, which lasts only two measures in the definitive version, has in the sketch a temporal duration equal to that of figure A, that is, four measures; it is set out beginning in the second measure of the third system and—literally repeated—extends to the first measure of the fourth system. In the definitive version Verdi completely eliminated the first two measures of this phrase, and he did so for a precise

EXAMPLE 4.3

Poco più animato
Zamoro
-rà! Mor - ran
morran
di mor - ti or - ren - de
Tenori
Coro
Mor - ran
mor - ran
mor-
Bassi
Mor - ran
mor - ran
mor-
tr
f
Z.
mor - ran
mor - ran
di mor - ti or - ren - de morran
mor - ran
mor - ran
mor-
ran
mor - ran
mor - ran
mor-
p

Example 4.3, *cont.*

EXAMPLE 4.3, *cont.*

reason: they are identical in rhythmic pattern to figure C, with whose threefold repetition the stretta concludes. From a definition of the sections we thus move to the more precise articulation of their relationships and so to a more effective—and dramatically more functional—working-out of their durations.

In the course of these few simple measures, we bear witness to an extraordinary process of clarification of musical ideas and to their masterly and economical deployment in the larger structure of a passage already clearly identified. The fact that the three measures that conclude the sketch become ten in the definitive version is of no importance, given that the final seven measures are nothing more than a temporal extension of the tonic chord, necessary for the proportions of the entire episode.

THE SECOND part of the sketch in the Gesellschaft der Musikfreunde contains a section of *Alzira* that is musically and dramatically remote from the end of the Prologue. This passage comes from the "Finale dell'Atto Primo," in particular the moment at which Gusmano, having discovered his beloved Alzira in the arms of his rival Zamoro, is about to order his soldiers to lead Zamoro to the scaffold. The unexpected arrival of Alvaro, Gusmano's father, reverses the situation: the old "governatore del Perù" (as the cast list in the libretto describes Alvaro) recognizes that Zamoro is the warrior who in the Prologue had saved his life by rescuing him from torture and death at the hands of the Incas. The sketch begins after Zamoro's solo, at Gusmano's words "Udiste il cenno?" addressed to "the soldiers who are about to drag away Zamoro," and ends with the words (again Gusmano's) "E' destin ch'ei mora: oltre sfuggir non può" (see example 4.4).[15]

The central moment of the episode is Alvaro's recognition of Zamoro; and in order to characterize in the most telling musical terms this culminating point in the action, Verdi felt the need to define precisely, through this sketch, his musical ideas. As we have seen, the composer wanted, in the closing chorus of the Prologue, above all to establish the "texture" of the episode, the dimension of its musical space and, in the stretta, to measure and weigh the duration of and relationship among various phrases. Here, on the contrary, he needed to identify the musical means through which the dramatic tension would be constructed; the duration of the sketch exactly corresponds to that of the definitive version, and the musical material used is substantially the same. At this point in the action the two most important features are the progression that leads to the climax and then the unwinding of the tension thus created; these features are reflected in the two parts that constitute the episode. The watershed is marked by the choral exclamation "Fia ver!"—words that are, significantly, written out fully in the sketch, on the first measure of the seventh system. Once again a comparison with the libretto printed for the Naples premiere is instructive in that it contains a Cammarano's version of the text *before* Verdi had set the passage to music. In the libretto, Alzira's first exclamation is "No, crudi . . . no . . .," which is a more coherent reaction to the violence of the Spanish soldiers toward Zamoro, as prescribed by the stage direction. But this phrase is less singeable than the one that appears in the score, "Aita, o ciel..." The most important alteration, however, occurs in the exclamation at the center of the episode, the "Fia ver!" According to Cammarano's version, this was to be sung by Gusmano alone; Verdi gave it instead to the chorus, partly to add musical force to the "viva sorpresa" required by the stage direction, but mostly to underline with a clear dynamic gesture the culminating point of the episode, the pivotal dramatic moment whose precise working out gave rise to this part of the sketch.

In Cammarano's libretto, this episode formed a unit with the preceding passage, Zamoro's impassioned solo "Teco sperai combattere," since the poetic meter (*settenari*, varying between *sdruccioli*, *piani*, and *tronchi*) is the same.

EXAMPLE 4.4

(ai soldati che muovonsi in atto di trascinar Zamoro)
Gusmano
U - di - ste il cen - no?
Alzira
A - i - ta, o ciel...
Vi - vc Za - mo - ro, e il
G.
Com - pia - si.
Alvaro
Che fu?
Alz.
bar - ba - ro spen - to lo vuol...
Alv.
Chi veg - gio!... è
p

Alv.
des - so, è quel ma - gna - ni - mo a cui la vi - ta io
G.
Fia
Soprani
Fia
Tenori
(viva sorpresa in tutti)
Fia
Bassi
Fia
Coro
p
Alv.
deg - gio!...
Alz. (ad Alvaro)
Pie - ta - de im - plo - ra...
G.
ver!...
ver!...
ver!...
ver!...
ff
p
ppp

EXAMPLE 4.4, *cont.*

Verdi, however, wanted to separate the episode from its surroundings clearly and with a decisive gesture. To this end nothing was more functional than transferring the articulation from the voices to the orchestra. The two parts that make up the episode are each characterized by a persistent rhythmic figure in the bass (the only element—apart from the voices—to be notated in the sketch); and the use of this figure is all the more revealing in that the harmonies of these two basses are far from obvious in the definitive orchestral version. But even in this episode, which could in no sense be classified as one of the opera's "closed" forms, the need for formal equilibrium has a decisive function: Verdi needed twelve measures in order to bring the tension to its point of incandescence, and just the same number, characterized by the pulsating figure of octave leaps in the bass, ♪ 𝄾 ♪ 𝄾 ♪ 𝄾 ♪ 𝄾 | to define the sense of total suspension resulting from the recognition. What is more, the progress of the voices is notated as an uninterrupted flow, a temporal continuum that is set against, and out of phase with, the inexorable bass ostinato; to the point that Verdi failed to indicate the vocal changes of clef, and the sketch is therefore comprehensible only if one has the libretto—or, better still, the definitive version—at hand.

Alvaro's next phrase, "Nella polve genuflesso," begins the finale proper; the articulation returns to the vocal parts, adapting itself to the text as conceived by Cammarano (ottonari set out in double quatrains for each character) and to a symmetrical aligning of musical phrases suited to the "closed number" and to the stasis of the action.

If compared with the *I due Foscari* fragment discussed in chapter 4, this sketch for *Alzira* documents an earlier creative phase—a moment that I would venture to suggest coincides with Verdi's very first musical conception; and it also reveals that, already during the period in which this opera was composed (the first half of 1845) Verdi's primary intention was to create a continuity in the unfolding of the dramatic discourse and, above all, to work out the durational relationships between the various sections and then the manner in which these could be characterized by musical elements. The Vienna sketch is a "continuity draft" in the sense that everything put down on the page precisely establishes the flow of the musico-dramatic discourse and its temporal articulation; the sketch enabled Verdi to fix the gradual progression, the various stages of dramatic development, saving for a later phase the elaboration and defining of details. What in *Macbeth* will encompass the entire unfolding of the score is already prefigured in the formal equilibrium that characterizes the score of *Alzira*. At the same time, in this phase in his development as a musical dramatist Verdi was not yet ready to conceive the uninterrupted unfolding of the musical design across an entire drama, the kind of musico-dramatic conception shown us in emblematic form by the *Rigoletto* sketch. During the period in which he composed *Alzira*, the temporal dimension that he wanted to fix with precision was that of a single episode, such as the concluding chorus of the Prologue, or else that of a dramatically relevant moment such as Alvaro's recognition of Zamoro—a moment that has an important function in the development of the entire action. But, even though the scale was comparatively restricted, it is as well to underline how these two moments, dramatically and musically so distant from each other, both required Verdi to elaborate on paper; in the overall economy of the composing process they are thus equivalent, and in their equivalence—above all if we consider them in the historical perspective of Italian opera—lies the defining element of Verdi's new poetics.

THE INFORMATION offered by the Vienna sketch does not quite end here; an interesting corollary is supplied us by its brief external history, which will help us to understand the position that Verdi the artist already occupied in the European musical scene at the time that he wrote it. The autograph in the library of the Gesellschaft der Musikfreunde is part of a collection once belonging to Aloys Fuchs (1799–1853),[16] the nineteenth-century antiquarian and writer on music who in 1846, barely a year after the premiere of *Alzira*, decided to donate it to the Viennese institution, on whose advisory board he had served since 1829. Some lines written on the right-hand side of the recto tell us through which channel the autograph arrived in the Fuchs collection: "I certify from definite knowledge and from a comparison with other original writings of Maestro Verdi in my possession that both the notes and the words inscribed on this page are by the said Maestro. Naples 28 August 1846. Mass[eangelo] Masseangeli." From the "Brevi cenni sulla vita dell'abate Masseangelo Dottor Masseangeli," printed at the beginning of the catalog of musical manuscripts left by him in his will to the Accademia Filarmonica of Bologna,[17] we discover that in 1837 this learned antiquarian from Lucca "moved to Naples as tutor to the sons of the Prince of Monte Mileto and stayed there for eleven years, until 1848 [. . .]. In Naples he formed friendships with all those from his native city and with other Tuscans, good numbers of whom were earning their living in the same way he was; he also knew the most distinguished Neapolitans, and as many illustrious foreigners as visited the city."[18] Verdi must have figured among the latter: it may even be that Masseangeli owned ten or more of the composer's autographs because, again on the recto but on the left-hand side of the page and in Masseangeli's hand, we find the indication "N° 10."

The catalog of the Bologna collection lists other verdiana: an undated letter to Giovanni Ricordi from Paris, which undoubtedly comes from the period of Verdi's first visit to the French capital during the staging of *Jérusalem*; an album folio containing the beginning of the final trio of *Ernani*; and, most interesting in the present context, a "Piano *sketch* of the overture to the opera *Alzira*. (An extremely precious autograph.)."[19] A further sketch concerning this opera has recently come to light in the United States, and it is likely that this also came from the Masseangeli collection.[20]

We can only guess at how the Verdi autograph was transferred from the Masseangeli to the Fuchs collection, but a further piece of information in the Bolognese catalog points us to the most likely explanation. In the entry on "MOZART Wolfango Amedeo, second son of the great musician" we find listed among the autographs a "transcription of the Latin text of the *Credo*, authenticated by signor *Aloisio Fuchs* of Vienna,"[21] an authentication very similar to that sketched by Masseangeli on the Verdi autograph. The two men must have been in direct personal contact and swapped pieces from their collections; such exchanges were a common occurrence among collectors of rare items, as is testified, so far as Masseangeli is concerned, by numerous letters concerning the exchange of autographs.[22]

However, aside from this chronicle of nineteenth-century antiquarians, it is interesting to note how, already at the time of *Alzira*, the figure of Verdi had assumed—on a European level—an almost mythic dimension and that his name was considered worthy of being placed beside the most illustrious figures of his time and of the past.

Notes

1. For a first identification of this system of "signs" and of the three levels—dramatic, verbal, and musical—on which it is realized, see chapter 5. When the latter appeared in English, it was accompanied by two further articles that sought to develop the same ideas: see Pierluigi Petrobelli, William Drabkin, and Roger Parker, "Verdi's *Trovatore*: A Symposium," *Music Analysis* 1 (1982): 125–67. For a more systematic account of the issues, see chapter 6.

2. *L'abbozzo del Rigoletto di Giuseppe Verdi*, edizione fuori commercio a cura del Ministero della Cultura Popolare (Milan, 1941). This sketch has been relatively little discussed: a first, pioneering study was undertaken by Gino Roncaglia, "L'*abbozzo* del *Rigoletto*," in his *Galleria verdiana* (Milan, 1959), 87–100; I myself examine certain issues in chapter 3 (see especially pp. 59–71); Martin Chusid considers others in "Rigoletto and Monterone: A Study in Musical Dramaturgy," in *Report of the Eleventh Congress [of the International Musicological Society]* (Copenhagen, 1972), 325–35; see also the same author's preface to the critical edition of *Rigoletto* (Chicago and Milan, 1983), vii–viii. The most complete study of the sketch is Claudio Danuser, "Studien zu den Skizzen von Verdi's *Rigoletto*," (Ph.D. dissertation, Universität Bern, 1985).

3. See pp. 51–59.

4. See p. 71.

5. I had an opportunity to study the original document briefly in September 1982 and March 1986; during the intervening period, and subsequently, I have made use of a photographic reproduction.

6. Shelf mark: IV 66875. The page measures 31.6 cm. high by 23.5 cm. wide; in the lower part there is a watermark that I have not been able to identify; it is preserved in a bluish cover, on which is written "*Originale* / di / *Giuseppe Verdi*," underneath which appears "Für die Sammlung der / Musik-Verein in Wien / übergeben von / Aloys Fuchs

/ 1846." I should like to thank most cordially the library of the Gesellschaft der Musikfreunde in Vienna, its director, Dr. Otto Biba, and Herr Rhythus for the great courtesy shown me during my study of the autograph and for permission to reproduce it here in facsimile.

7. See G. Verdi, *Alzira*, Tragedia lirica in un Prologo e due Atti di Salvadore Cammarano . . . Canto e pianoforte, Milan, Ricordi, pl. no. 53706; the chorus is on pp. 30–34, the stretta on pp. 35–36. In the autograph full score, housed in the Ricordi archives of Milan, the coro and stretta occur in vol. 1 from fol. 46^{v} to fol. 52^{v}.

8. See Julian Budden, *The Operas of Verdi*, vol. 1 (London, 1973), 226.

9. ALZIRA. *Tragedia lirica.* Divisa in *Prologo* e due atti . . . da rappresentarsi nel Teatro S. Carlo, Napoli, dalla Tipografia Flautina, 1845, p. 8. A copy of this libretto is housed in the library of the Istituto nazionale di studi verdiani at Parma.

10. This interjection was originally in the following rhythm: [𝄾] ♪♪ (triplet [3]) ♩ ♩ .

11. Significantly, in the autograph score on fol. 47^{r-v}, Verdi wrote two measures of the pitches (but not the words) of Zamoro's interjection also on the staff reserved for the choral tenors. These two measures were later scratched away but are nevertheless still clearly legible.

12. It is hardly fortuitous that from the thirteenth to the twenty-sixth measure of the sketch, Verdi annotated fully, in repeated eighth-note triplets, the harmony of this modulatory passage.

13. In the section covered by the sketch I have added in square brackets those parts of the text for which there is music but no words, taking the latter from the definitive version of the score.

14. The pattern in the sketch also appears as an early version in the autograph score, later canceled by Verdi; see fols. 50^{v} and 51^{r}.

15. See the vocal score of *Alzira*, 87–89.

16. See O. Wessely's entry on Fuchs in *The New Grove Dictionary of Music and Musicians*, ed. Stanley Sadie (London, 1980), vol. 7, 1–2.

17. *Catalogo della collezione d'autografi lasciata alla R. Accademia Filarmonica di Bologna dall'accademico Ab. Dott. Masseangelo Masseangeli* . . . (Bologna, Regia Tipografia, 1881), xiii–xv. My thanks to Oscar Mischiati for pointing out the existence of these "Brevi cenni."

18. Ibid., xiii.

19. Ibid., 420.

20. Philip Gossett, who kindly informed me of the existence of this sketch, will discuss it in a forthcoming article.

21. *Catalogo*, 147–48.

22. See, for example, ibid., 101.

CHAPTER 5

TOWARD AN EXPLANATION OF THE DRAMATIC STRUCTURE OF *IL TROVATORE*

TRANSLATED BY WILLIAM DRABKIN

El sueño de la razón produce monstruos
Goya

In no other of Verdi's operas does one find even the slightest inclination toward humor. And now the old master writes a work that gives his whole past the lie, so to speak, an *opera buffa* raised to the *nth* power, the sublime example of its kind. *Falstaff* throws a light back over all of Verdi's previous work. It changes the aspect of this work; there must be more to it than we believed; the master who could create such an opera did not write *Trovatore* as mere hand organ music. And, indeed, the brightest ones among us have already come to the conclusion that Verdi's secret (I am not now speaking of the so-called secrets of form) lies as deep as Wagner's, and is much less obvious than is that of the calculating Wagner—rationalizing sometimes to the point of excess.[1]

WITH THESE words Alfred Einstein concluded the section on Verdi in his "Opus Ultimum," an essay that explores the very last work of each of the major figures of music history. Perhaps the great musicologist, whose penetrating insights were equaled only by his ability to capture the essence of a genre or a historical moment, did not fully realize the breadth or profundity of his observations, particularly of their force when applied to the music itself. Of course, we are still a long way from identifying, confidently and with absolute precision, the formal principles according to which Verdi's scores were composed and the structural laws they obey. Surely their amazing richness—testified to by our continuous rediscovery of values and meanings in these works, which have been with us for quite some time—cannot be explained in

The translator gratefully acknowledges the assistance of Roger Parker and Pierluigi Petrobelli.

any other way than through the presence of formal principles whose determining power is directly related to, and measured by, the manifold and complex relations it establishes.[2]

All this becomes clear when we try to identify the principles underlying the construction of a score like *Il trovatore*: for neither the psychological-musical portrayal of the characters nor their development during the unfolding of the plot can be called upon to explain its structure. We are accustomed to considering *Rigoletto*, *Il trovatore*, and *La traviata* as belonging to the same stylistic moment, as though the mere dates of composition were sufficient to unify their musical characteristics, which are assumed to remain constant in the three operas. But even if we limit our observations to the dynamics of the plot, we cannot fail to be struck by the complexity and extraordinary amount of psychological characterization of the two operas based on French plays and, on the other hand, by the almost complete lack of all this in the opera based on García Gutiérrez's drama. In *Rigoletto* and *La traviata* the plots are directional, that is, the characters develop and interact with one another following the course of events. By contrast, the plot of *Il trovatore* is static, since none of the characters "grow" in any way during its four acts. As Gabriele Baldini has explained:

> One can say of no other Verdi opera that the libretto fails to narrate; any attempt to run over the events of the plot very soon becomes meaningless because they all cancel each other out and become confused in the memory. It is a very special quality of this distinguished text, and derives not so much from individual complications as from the extremely elusive nature of the characters and events outside their musical setting.[3]

The cohesion and the enhancing power of the opera must therefore be found exclusively in the music, or, to be more precise, in the constructive principles and relationships that the composer establishes in the score.

Let us return for a moment to our comparison of *Rigoletto* and *La traviata* with *Il trovatore*. In the first two works, there is not always a neat and simple distinction between closed forms (arias, ensembles, choruses—i.e., sections in which a self-contained musical organization corresponds precisely to a closed metrical structure in the text) and passages in which a gradual definition of the psychological growth of a character leads to the elimination of such symmetries and congruities, or at least to the absence of musically self-contained sections. In *Il trovatore*, musical "connectives" (including the introductory orchestral passages) have been reduced to a minimum, and the essence of the discourse is concentrated in forms that are completely self-contained. This musical situation corresponds precisely to what we find in the dramatic articulation of the opera. Of all Verdi's scores, *Il trovatore* is the least bound to the *parola scenica*, the "scenic word" that defines or shapes a situation, even when such a word—a true verbal *Leitmotiv*—recurs several times during the action. A typical example of this is the exclamation "Mi vendica!" which occurs several times in the opera (vocal score, pp. 63, 69, 72, 84) and is meant to identify what Verdi calls Azucena's *amor filiale*, one of the two poles about which her personality is built;[4] but apart from its rhythmic scansion, this exclamation lacks any independent or recurring musical shape by which we can identify it. In the score of *Il trovatore*, it is therefore of greatest importance to consider the musical elements in their own right, ignoring their power to define the psychological situation of a character, and giving still less consideration to the thoughts which that character may express. What *is* significant is how these musical elements are placed within the organically self-contained sections, as well as their recurrence in the course of the opera; from this it follows that the concepts of "duration" and of the articulation of the whole into parts are fundamental to the opera:

> As in all great works of art, different sections of *Il trovatore* are of variable density, and are distributed and juxtaposed within an extremely careful architectural design. The four-part structure, which is itself intended to underline the symmetries, is emphasised by the fact that each part is divided into two. Furthermore, even the durations are calculated in mirror image. The first and third acts are shorter and slighter than the second and fourth, so the opera can usefully be divided into two parts which gradually move towards more complex, daring organisms.[5]

VERDI'S ENCOUNTER with Shakespeare in *Macbeth* was invaluable to him not only as a man of the theater but also—and to exactly the same extent—as a musician. He gradually became aware of the need to relate systematically the various points in the score with a musical coherence that would correspond to the coherence on the dramatic level. And so, if the articulation of the drama and of the "durations" in *Il trovatore* is so rich in precise relationships and carefully balanced parallelisms, then we should also expect to find a corresponding organic unity in the score. Moreover, if the psychological makeup of a character and his behavior and development are irrelevant in this score, that is, if the theatrical dynamic of the opera is based on the conflict between fixed, "affective" situations (in the Baroque sense), then the maximum simplicity, clarity, and elementariness become the *conditiones sine quibus non* of its success. The fact that, upon superficial hearing, this music can sound like "mere hand-organ music," far from being a defect, becomes instead an indispensable ingredient of its success. The components of the musical discourse *must* be elementary because they must have maximum functionality; and this elemental quality becomes a dramatic necessity.

Indeed, a penetrating and detailed study of the score of the opera reveals that the relationships and symmetries at the musical level are just as numerous as those on the dramatic level that Baldini so acutely described. The complexity of these relationships is such that, for Verdi, only a few fixed points are needed to organize the score; and the number of individual elements of the musical language that is needed is surprisingly small. But what are these elements about which the relationships and symmetries are established? In practice there is not a single one, from the simplest to the most complex, that escapes this game of relationships.

Certainly one of the simplest elements consists of "sonorities." By the term "sonority" I mean a specific pitch prolonged by various means of articulation and considered independently of any harmonic function it may imply as a result of being heard in a particular context. That such sonorities were of enormous importance in Verdi's musical thinking has, I believe, been demonstrated in an earlier article of mine, where I showed that the complex four-part polyphonic string texture in the opening bars of Act III of *Rigoletto* was initially sketched as an octave sonority on E in a middle register (*e–e′*); the polyphonic elaboration of this sonority is a kind of "translation"—a complex one, to be sure, but one that always allows us to perceive the original pitch matrix.[6] This constructive principle of Verdi's can also be found in much larger structures, such as entire episodes within a scene or "set number." And it can be recognized (certainly from *Macbeth* onward) as a way of drawing together different parts of a score. This musical element is thus itself an element of dramatic articulation, an ideal instrument of pure theater, as Artaud understood it.

The documentation of the genesis of *Il trovatore*, though scant, nevertheless enables us to recognize that the starting-point of Verdi's interest in García Gutiérrez's play was the character of Azucena: "I would like two women. The principal one is the gipsy (*la gitana*), a strange character after whom the opera should be named; the other would be a *comprimaria*."[7] While the libretto was being worked out, Verdi sent Cammarano (who was basically indifferent toward the "new" plot) precise instructions in order that the librettist might be made aware of how he (Verdi) conceived the character:

> Unless I am mistaken, it seems to me that certain situations lack the force and originality that they had before, and that—most important of all—Azucena has lost her strange and new personality; it seems to me that this woman's two great passions, *amor filiale* and *amor materno*, are no longer presented with their maximum force.[8]

And farther on in the same letter:

> Do not make Azucena a mad woman. Broken down by fatigue, sorrow, terror, and wakefulness, she is incapable of speaking coherently. Her feelings are overwhelmed, but she is not crazy. *We must maintain until the very end the two great passions of this woman*: her love for Manrique and her desperate need to avenge her mother.[9]

Azucena is thus portrayed as a two-sided character. And around this ambivalence the entire dramatic action ultimately revolves.

For Verdi it was necessary to assert this point of departure in a very obvious way, to present it with the utmost clarity to the spectator and to fix it in his mind. Using a traditional procedure of the theater, the evocation of a principal character by a dialogue among the characters on stage, García Gutiérrez evokes the image of the gipsy woman (and, at the same time, all that has occurred before the play begins) in a dialogue among three servants of the count of Luna: Guzman, Ferrando, and old Jimeno. Following the conventions of melodrama,[10] Verdi replaces this dialogue with a narration given by one of the attendants (Ferrando) to the chorus. This narration in fact takes the form of a two-strophe Ballata that, by being placed at this point in the action, has direct precedents in operatic tradition—not the Italian tradition, however, but French and German ones.[11] (We may observe, in passing, how smoothly Verdi grafted a stylistic experience originating beyond the Alps onto the stock of his own native tradition.) Thus the Ballata has the same function as the prologue in ancient Classical tragedy (indeed, Verdi calls the entire episode simply "Introduzione") with the bass-voice Ferrando assuming the role of choryphaeus who evokes emotional responses from the chorus.[12]

The "sonority" that Verdi associates with Azucena is B. It is established as early as m. 21 (vocal score, p. 2, systems 1–2), after the opening fanfare, and articulated for a full eight bars up to Ferrando's cry "All'erta! all'erta!," which is also declaimed on B. In this position—and bearing in mind the function of this note in the general plan of the score—the cry seems directed not so much "at the retainers who are nearly falling asleep" as at the spectator, as if to involve him in the plot by pointing out a basic element of the dramatic action.

The subsequent brief interventions by the chorus evoke two more dynamic elements of the plot: the count's jealousy (see mm. 43–46: vocal score, p. 3, systems 1–2), which is delineated chiefly by the rhythmic figure ♬ ♩. and repeated persistently,[13] and the figure of Garzia/Manrico, presented here by means of the articulation of the note G (mm. 51–59; vocal score, pp. 3–4). But these two interjections are not elaborated: they function primarily as simple declarations (albeit capable of later development) and are exposed at this time merely to bring the polarity of Azucena into greater relief.

The two symmetrical strophes of Ferrando's Ballata open with "an Andante mosso of fourteen bars in common time,"[14] which is constructed along exactly the same lines as the poetic text: three phrases, each comprising two lines, which are arranged in an ascending progression. The range and movement of the progression is—certainly not by chance—from B to b, and the last line ("e chi trova d'accanto a quel bambino") is declaimed at the higher of these pitches. We thus get a further articulation of the sonority of B,[15] which reaches its maximum tension here with the help of chromatic movement in the orchestral accompaniment (vocal score, bottom of p. 5).

A sonority is defined more completely if it becomes associated with a tonality, that is, if tonal tension or release is explicitly indicated. In the case we are examining, the sonority of B can function as the fifth degree of E minor (or major) or the third of G major. Abramo Basevi, observant as ever, had already noticed the dramatic function of these two keys in *Il trovatore* when he wrote, with specific reference to the Allegretto from Ferrando's Ballata, that "in the first period in E minor, and the second in G major, Verdi has followed the system of *musical economy*, about which I have spoken elsewhere."[16] Nevertheless, in order to understand the precise dramatic function of the two keys by which Azucena's ambivalence is realized in musical terms, it would be worthwhile calling the reader's attention to a few other characteristics of Verdi's style. Independently of the formal organization of set numbers, determined in most instances by the structure of the poetic text (whereby a poetic quatrain corresponds to a melodic "arch" form, the greatest tension being reached in the section corresponding to the third line),[17] Verdi's musical language at times takes on a special configuration of its characteristic elements in connection with a specific expression or verbal symbol, which is given maximum significance by being translated by the composer into musical terms. This is, in effect, what Luigi Dallapiccola has defined as the *ideogramma musicale*, or musical image.[18] And it is interesting to note how this symbolism is preserved precisely and consistently throughout Verdi's career.[19] At other times, however, a specific term or word becomes the critical point from which the entire articulation of the musical argument springs forth; that is, the word becomes the element on which the spectator's attention must be focused. And we can observe that it is sometimes actually divorced from the situation on stage or the dramatic relevance of the moment. An example of the latter case occurs precisely in the first Allegretto section of Ferrando's Ballata, where the focal words are "zingara" (gipsy woman) and "fanciullo" (little boy), the respective objects of Azucena's *amor filiale* and *amor materno*. These two words correspond to the two tonalities associated with this character, with which we are presented in turn: E minor and G major, rotating around the sonority of B. In this way Azucena's ambivalence, hinted at rather than stated explicitly, takes on a superhuman dimension. And the spectral world—inhabited by whispers, by flying nocturnal animals, and by mortal fears—from which she and her mother originate can be realized musically in all its terrifying force in the Allegro assai agitato that concludes the "Introduzione." This final episode represents the dynamic projection of the gipsy's world, still in its early stages but susceptible to important developments later in the score.

After all that has been said up to now, it is easy to see why the musical image of the flame which burns and consumes always appears at the same pitch level in the score: it is nothing other than the simplest, most direct articulation of the sonority of B (example 5.1). Placed emphatically at the head of Azucena's Canzone in Act II (vocal score, p. 58, system 2; and p. 62, system 3), it enables us to interpret the Canzone itself as an ingenious elaboration of that note. The figure recurs in Act II—at the same pitch—in the middle of Azucena's Racconto (vocal score, pp. 70–71), and once more at the beginning of the finale of Act IV, when she describes to Manrico, for the last time, the spectacle of her mother's torture (vocal score, p. 227).

Example 5.1

The Racconto in Act II lacks a formally symmetrical design for the very reason that its character is not contemplative or lyrical but rather narrative and thus dynamic. (Thus it differs from the Canzone, which is divided into two musically equivalent strophes, though the musical content of the Canzone and the Racconto are conceptually and even substantially the same.) It stands in the same relation to the Canzone as the Allegro assai agitato that concludes the first scene of the opera does to Ferrando's Ballata. And it is certainly not by chance that these two parts of the opera have exactly the same key scheme—E minor moving to A minor—or that the evocation of the principal character of the scene is followed by his appearance on stage. But the precise relation between these two parts of the drama is already explained to the ear of the spectator by means of a tonal identity.

In this freely organized Racconto the moments in which Azucena's "passions" erupt become the most conspicuous. At the words "Ei distruggeasi in pianto" (he [Manrico] was beside himself with tears) not only does the key of G major return with perfect definition but also the rhythmic figure that is always associated with Manrico (see the figure on p. 108) appears in the vocal line. By contrast, the evocation of the image of Azucena's burnt mother, beginning pianissimo with a pedal on B in the first violins, is completed and resolved in E minor by the second appearance of the figure associated with the flame.

The dramatic link between the "Introduzione" and Azucena's Racconto is further underlined by precise and timely rhythmic analogies (see examples 5.2, 5.3, and 5.4). The figure that runs through the entire Allegro assai agitato, the chorus "Sull'orlo dei tetti," at the end of the first scene, in which terror evokes

EXAMPLE 5.2

EXAMPLE 5.3

EXAMPLE 5.4

in the terrified servants' minds the very shapes into which the gipsy woman is monstrously transformed (vocal score, p. 16), recurs in a quite similar form throughout the first part of the Racconto (vocal score, p. 67), which, as I have said, is in the same key of A minor, and finally returns in Act III at the moment in which Ruiz reports to Manrico that Azucena has been taken prisoner by the count's followers and is to be led to the stake (vocal score, pp. 173–74).

The tonal ambivalence between E minor and G major helps to characterize Azucena also in Act III, when she speaks about the real life of a gipsy, and what the lost son means to her ("Giorni poveri vivea"; vocal score, pp. 152–53). But the explosion of motherly "passion," which is realized here in a passage in E major (example 5.5), gives rise to one of the most astonishing strokes in all Verdian drama: for this phrase is an almost literal transposition of the concluding phrase of each of the two strophes of Leonora's Act I Cavatina (vocal score, p. 24, system 3; and p. 26, system 1). Such an extraordinary parallelism can be explained only by theories of deeply unconscious motivation.

An unexpected confirmation—albeit in a negative manner—of the interpretation I have proposed here is suggested by the concluding section of Act III, scene 1 (example 5.6). Azucena, bound in chains by her persecutors, invokes

Example 5.5

Example 5.6

divine justice to defend her. This section is in the key of F major; none of the elements that are associated with her character appears there. The reason for this can be drawn from the dramatic situation: at this moment in the action Azucena is no longer a daughter or a mother, her two "passions" for the moment being overpowered by the more urgent, basic need for survival. Thus all her characteristic ambivalences are suppressed.

The use of "sonorities"—and, to a lesser extent, of keys—can be further illustrated in the score not only through Azucena but through all the other principal characters. All that I have said up to now has been intended mainly as an illustration of one of the procedures Verdi employs to bring unity to the score.

ANOTHER ELEMENT of the musical language that Verdi elaborates with amazing complexity to bring dramatic unity to the opera is that of rhythm. Only a systematic analysis could reveal precisely the quantity and nature of rhythmic components that serve the composer's purposes, and the number of different levels on which he uses them. For the moment let us look at just one example, the rhythmic figure associated with Manrico: . The four notes remain frequently, though not always, at the same pitch level. It is also significant that the figure does not change either in character or in the way it is notated, even when there is a change in meter. As I showed a little earlier, its first fleeting appearance occurs in the "Introduzione," in the second of the two brief interpolations that describe the old count of Luna's two sons, before Ferrando begins his Ballata; the figure occurs in the chorus at the words "la vera storia ci narra di Garzia" (tell us the true story of Garzia). The "true story" is about none other than Manrico, the son who was abducted by the gipsy woman and is now the object of Azucena's motherly love: hence the use of G major and the declamation on the note B (vocal score, p. 4, systems 1–2). This rhythmic figure returns, in the same key and likewise at the same pitch, in the middle of Azucena's Racconto at the words "Ei distruggeasi in pianto" (vocal score, p. 70, systems 2–3), as I have already noted. And the figure comes back once more, again in G major and on the note B, when Manrico comforts Azucena with "Riposa o madre" in their duet in Act IV (vocal score, pp. 230ff.); in fact it becomes a constant throughout the scene, the element that dynamically defines the dramatic situation. Azucena, at last satisfied in her motherly feelings, gradually accepts into her vocal line the rhythmic figure associated with Manrico, making it her own (example 5.7).

But the figure is also used to characterize Manrico in other parts of the opera. The most complex polyphonic passage in the score occurs in the finale of Act II, before the Allegro vivo at which Ruiz and Manrico's followers arrive; here the tenor's voice stands out from the others not only by its regular pulse but also because each of its melodic fragments begins with or consists solely of the rhyth-

EXAMPLE 5.7

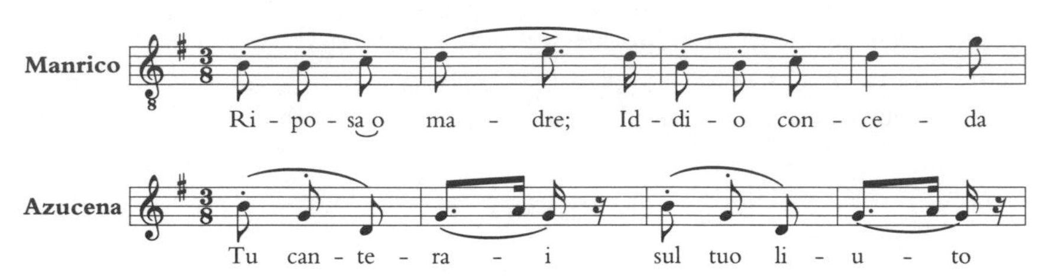

mic figure. The figure returns with an almost obsessive insistence in Manrico's Act III Cantabile, not only in the vocal part but also in the continual echo by the orchestral wind instruments (vocal score, pp. 169–71; see also the full score, pp. 295–98 in the Ricordi edition). There are, moreover, certain places at which the figure is present only because the composer intends an allusion to Manrico. For example, in the recitative preceding Leonora's Act IV aria (vocal score, p. 185, systems 3–4) the figure appears in an interjection by the violins, between phrases in the soprano part, as if to evoke the image of the person toward whom her expressions of love are directed. Perhaps the subtlest, most refined use of the figure is in the finale of Act II, where Leonora turns to Ines and the accompanying retinue of women, telling them that she wishes to abandon her worldly life and dedicate herself wholly to God. Actually, in order to express all this Leonora twice uses the rhythmic figure associated with Manrico (vocal score, p. 115, system 4). In this way, and with a simultaneity that is peculiar to musical theater, the character explains the reasons that circumstance obliges her to give and at the same time actually names the object of her true feelings.

ONLY A COMPREHENSIVE and systematic evaluation of the entire score can reveal the number of ways in which Verdi uses musical language to bring dramatic unity to the opera, and the number of levels on which unity is achieved; that will have to await another occasion. It has been my intention here simply to expose the problem methodologically and to test the usefulness of the analytical criteria on certain points in the score. Only after the completion of that large-scale study will it be possible to determine whether these formal principles are valid only for the score of *Il trovatore* or whether they are in fact stylistic constants that operate throughout Verdi's œuvre, or at least in his more mature works. The research carried out thus far seems to confirm, with surprising consistency, the validity of the second hypothesis; but, given the special nature of the dramatic substance of *Il trovatore*, its application to this opera assumes a form that is both extreme and unusual.

Finally, I consider it almost unnecessary to emphasize that my interpretation in no way pretends to offer a rigid, mechanical system of relationships and parallelism between dramatic actions and their musical expression. As Einstein rightly observed, "Verdi's secret . . . lies as deep as Wagner's, and is much less obvious." It has rather been my intention to single out certain principles at work in the score and to offer a rational explanation, based on the facts available, for the spontaneous and universal acclaim that the opera continues to enjoy.

Notes

1. Alfred Einstein, *Essays on Music* (New York, 1962), 87.

2. For the clarification of these ideas, and those that follow, I am grateful for the continued and lively debate I have enjoyed with colleagues, friends, and pupils. Thanks are due first of all to the students in the Ph.D. program in music at the City University of New York (in particular Daniel Sabbeth and Elliott Antokoletz) for their stimulating observations and discussions during the Verdi seminar in the autumn of 1970; also to Frits Noske and his seminar on *Otello* at the University of Amsterdam in the spring of 1971; and, last but not least, to Julian Budden.

3. Gabriele Baldini, *The Story of Giuseppe Verdi*, trans. Roger Parker (Cambridge, 1980), 210.

4. See Verdi's letter to Cammarano written on 9 April 1851, which I shall have occasion to refer to later. The letter is published in Gaetano Cesari and Alessandro Luzio, eds., *I copialettere di Giuseppe Verdi* (Milan, 1913), 118–21 (especially 118).

5. Baldini, *The Story of Giuseppe Verdi*, 213.

6. "Osservazioni sul processo compositivo in Verdi," *Acta musicologica* 43 (1971): 125–42 (especially 140–42); English translation in this book, chap. 4.

7. The text of this letter is quoted in Gino Monaldi, *Verdi: 1838–1898*, 4th edition (Milan, 1951), 141, where it is dated 2 January 1850. If this date is correct then we must suppose that Verdi's interest in García Gutiérrez's drama preceded the composition of *Stiffelio*. On this point, however, see Julian Budden, *The Operas of Verdi*, vol. 2 (London, 1978), 60.

8. Letter to Cammarano of 9 April 1851; *Copialettere*, 118.

9. *Copialettere*, 120.

10. To give just one example, the witches and the assassins of Banquo, who are given individual speaking roles in Shakespeare's *Macbeth*, are transformed in the opera into a female and male chorus, respectively, each of which expresses itself in the first person.

11. Examples of French grand opera that Verdi could have had in mind include Boieldieu's *La Dame blanche* and Meyerbeer's *Robert le diable*. In the German tradition, the idea of a ballad that contains the essence of the opera *in nuce* is realized in exemplary fashion in *Der fliegende Holländer*, the starting point for the composition of which was—according to Wagner's explicit recollections—Senta's ballad in Act II (see Ernest Newman, *Wagner as Man and Artist* [New York, 1960], 315); the position of the ballad in the structure of this opera is, nevertheless, irregular. I am indebted to the late Professor Oliver Strunk for these astute observations.

12. "This character [the bass] has an extremely anomalous role: he is placed at the beginning of the action and gathers together the drama at its lowest, most obscure and shadowy point, but then has no other important sections in the rest of the opera." In fact,

"after the first scene, which in some ways functions as a prelude, the bass leaves the character list." Baldini, *The Story of Giuseppe Verdi*, 216.

13. Note that the figure recurs precisely at the moments in which this "jealousy" explodes: in the finale of Act II, when the count enters, hoping to abduct Leonora from the convent (vocal score, 116: the rhythm of the figure is inverted); and in the Scena and duet in Act IV, when Leonora pleads with the count—and thereby excites his jealousy—to order Manrico's release (vocal score, 215, systems 2–4). The meaning of this figure is sometimes less obvious, more complex, e.g., at the words "con te per sempre unita nella tomba scenderò" in Leonora's Act IV Cabaletta "Tu vedrai che amore in terra" (vocal score, 199 and 202), where the figure is used to indicate that the count's jealousy poses a direct threat to Leonora and, ultimately, will be the reason for her death.

14. Abramo Basevi, *Studio sulle opere di Giuseppe Verdi* (Florence, 1859), 206.

15. Even in the second of the chorus's interjections it occurs no less frequently (see mm. 53–56; vocal score, 4, systems 1–2).

16. Basevi, *Studio sulle opere di Giuseppe Verdi*, 206. But see also pp. 210–11, where Basevi "demonstrates" why Verdi has correctly harmonized "Stride la vampa."

17. For a demonstration of how this formal principle is specifically applied to nineteenth-century Italian opera, see Luigi Dallapiccola, "Words and Music in Italian Nineteenth-Century Opera"; see chap. 1, n. 31.

18. Luigi Dallapiccola, "Per una rappresentazione de 'Il ritorno di Ulisse in patria' di Claudio Monteverdi," *Musica*, vol. 2 (Florence, 1943), 129.

19. I will give just two examples. The act of rowing is realized in musical terms by means of a bass ostinato whose prominent feature is an acciaccatura based on the semitone below the main note: *Alzira*, Act I, at the words "Di Gusman su fragil barca" in the recitative preceding the protagonist's aria; *Stiffelio*, Act I, scene 2, throughout the protagonist's Racconto (consisting of two symmetrical strophes) which begins with the words "Di qua varcando sul primo albore." Verdi realizes the idea of the sun, or some other shining light, with a long-held trill in a high register in the violins or the flute: *La forza del destino*, Act I, at Don Alvaro's words "E quando il sole, nume dell'India"; *Aida*, Act I, at the end of Radamès's Romanza at the words "un trono vicino al sol"; and here in *Il trovatore* in the recitative preceding Leonora's Act I aria, at the words "Come d'aurato sogno."

CHAPTER 6

MUSIC IN THE THEATER (APROPOS OF *AIDA*, ACT III)

To Nicola LeFanu

IN OPERA, various "systems" work together, each according to its own nature and laws, and the result of the combination is much greater than the sum of the individual forces. In this essay I wish to discuss the interaction of the three main systems—dramatic action, verbal organization, and music. The dramatic action unfolds the events of the plot; the verbal organization, structured most of the time in lines and verses, offers support and definition to the action; and the music interprets and transforms, in its own terms, both action and text. I may add that by "music" I mean not only the musical declamation of the text but also the orchestral part(s) along with it. Musical theater involves the interaction of these three systems. But how does the chemical compounding take place? And what is the nature of the bonding?

Rather than expound abstract theories, I prefer to allow the basic principles to emerge from a specific example, and shall consider the first part of the third act of *Aida*; only at the end of this essay I shall suggest some conclusions—which I shall offer for discussion and development.

Let me start by summarizing the situation at that point in the opera.[1] It is nighttime on a bank of the Nile. Amneris, daughter of the pharaoh, and the high priest Ramfis enter on a barge. Amneris is betrothed to Radamès, a young but already victorious Egyptian captain, and she has come to pray at the temple on the eve of her wedding. Aida is an Ethiopian princess held in slavery by the Egyptians; she is in love with Radamès and is afraid of being abandoned by him. She dreams of Ethiopia but fears that she will never see it again. Her father, King Amonasro, is, in disguise, also a prisoner of the Egyptians: he is planning revenge and wants Aida to obtain from Radamès the secret of the Egyptian plan to attack Ethiopia. Aida is forced to yield by the psychological violence inflicted on her by her father, who then hides himself so that he may spy on the lovers.

This part of the plot is articulated in three distinct episodes: the entrance of Amneris and Ramfis, Aida's monologue, and the exchange between Aida and her father. These episodes, however, do not have equal importance. Underlying the entire opera there are some basic conflicts: one between the feelings and the aspirations of the individuals, and the interests of the state and the religious establishment; the other within each of the two protagonists (Aida and Radamès) between their mutual love and the love for their own country. Because of these conflicts, not only are Aida and Radamès in the end crushed but Amneris is as well. These conflicts explain why, in the scenes we are analyzing, Aida weeps over her country rather than over her lover; and also why Amneris and Ramfis do not take part in the action here but are absorbed in the Nile landscape until the end of the act: none of the conflicts concern them at this point of the dramatic action. Aida is in a totally different situation; she is alone and motionless, but her inner conflict and especially her desperate longing for her homeland will set this part of the tragedy in motion.

All this is clearly discernible in the structure of the lines created by Ghislanzoni, the author of the libretto, under Verdi's watchful eye.[2] While the dialogue between Amneris and Ramfis is in plain, traditional recitative meter—eleven- and seven-syllable lines freely alternated—the episode in which Aida expresses the basic "affect" of the situation consists of two quatrains of eleven-syllable lines alternately *piani* and *tronchi*[3] and with alternate rhymes:

O cieli azzurri... o dolci aure native
Dove sereno il mio mattin brillò...
O verdi colli... o profumate rive...
O patria mia, mai più ti rivedrò!

O fresche valli... o queto asil beato
Che un dì promesso dall'amor mi fu...
Ahimè! d'amore il sogno è dileguato...
O patria mia, non ti vedrò mai più! (Lines 21–28)

The dialogue between Amonasro and Aida, on the other hand, is articulated in various sections; each of them is a well-calculated step forward in the crescendo of dramatic tension, and the verbal structure is clearly differentiated with respect to meter and rhyme; it can be summarized as follows:

1. Amonasro informs Aida that he knows all her feelings, and he lists them: love for Radamès, rivalry with Amneris, pride in her royal origin, longing to return to their country (lines 29–38). Eleven- and seven-syllable lines are freely alternated in recitative style and concluded with a *rima baciata* (lines 37–38), the usual device in the libretto technique to indicate the closing of a section. After this recitative the duet proper begins.
2. Amonasro: "Aida will be able to see her country again" (lines 39–46). There are two quatrains of eleven-syllable lines with alternate rhymes *piane* and *tronche*, each of them stemming from a couple of lines to Amonasro, immediately echoed by a couple to Aida:

Amonasro Rivedrai le foreste imbalsamate...
Le nostre valli... i nostri templi d'òr!...
Aida Rivedrò le foreste imbalsamate...
Le nostre valli... i nostri templi d'òr...
Amonasro Sposa felice a lui che amasti tanto,
Tripudi immensi ivi potrai gioir...
Aida Un giorno solo di sì dolce incanto...
Un'ora di tal gaudio[4]... e poi morir!

3. "The cruel Egyptians have invaded and soiled their beloved country" (lines 47–54). Again, there are two quatrains of eleven-syllable lines, with the same structure as the two previous ones, a quatrain to Amonasro (lines 47–50) and a quatrain to Aida (lines 51–54), which echoes that of Amonasro:

Amonasro Pur rammenti che a noi l'Egizio immite
Le case, i templi e l'are profanò...
Trasse in ceppi le vergini rapite...
Madri... vecchi e fanciulli ei trucidò.
Aida Ah! ben rammento quegli infausti giorni,
Rammento i lutti che il mio cor soffrì...
Deh! fate o Numi che per noi ritorni
L'alba invocata dei sereni dì.

4. "The time of revenge has come; everything is ready, but for the discovery of the military secret" (lines 55–58). There is a quatrain of eleven-syllable lines to Amonasro, alternately *piani* and *tronchi*:

Amonasro Non fia che tardi—In armi ora si desta
Il popol nostro—tutto pronto è già...
Vittoria avrem... Solo a saper mi resta
Qual sentiero il nemico seguirà...

Sections 2, 3, and 4 form a unity in themselves since they all stem from quatrains of eleven-syllable lines, each line being alternately *piano* and *tronco* with alternating rhymes. It is the very same structure of meter and rhyme scheme as Aida's monologue (lines 21–28). The "affect" expressed there, the longing for her country, is structurally brought forward and the dramatic function is developed to a maximum.

5. Amonsaro finally reveals his scheme: it is up to Aida to get from Radamès the military secret; Aida refuses violently (lines 59–62). These are four eleven-syllable lnes of recitative, *liberi*.
6. Amonsaro: "Let then the Egyptians come to destroy our country"; Aida is terrified (lines 63–72). There are two quatrains of six-syllable lines

(*intrecciate* thus: a *rima piana* at the second and sixth lines, and a *rima tronca* at the fourth and eighth lines), plus a couplet of six-syllable lines, the second rhyming with the previous *rima tronca*:

Amonasro Su, dunque! sorgete
Egizie coorti!
Col fuoco struggete
Le nostre città...

Spargete il terrore,
Le stragi, le morti...
Al vostro furore
Più freno non v'ha.

Aida Ah padre!...
Amonasro Mia figlia
Ti chiami!...
Aida Pietà!

7. "The Egyptians will raid Ethiopia" (lines 73–78). A sestet of seven-syllable lines, alternately *sdruccioli* without rhyme and *piani* with rhyme, is concluded by a *verso tronco*:

Amonasro Flutti di sangue scorrono
Sulle città dei vinti...
Vedi?... dai negri vortici
Si levano gli estinti...
Ti additan essi e gridano:
Per te la patria muor!

8. "The ghost of Aida's mother will come to curse her" (lines 79–84). Again a sestet of seven-syllable lines, but with the second and third lines rhyming *a rima baciata* ("affaccia"/"braccia") and the fourth and sixth lines connected by assonance to the *rima tronca* of the previous sestet ("muòr"/"levò"/"Ah! no"):

Aida Pietà...
Amonasro Una larva orribile
Fra l'ombre a noi s'affaccia...
Trema! Le scarne braccia
Sul capo tuo levò...
Tua madre ell'è... ravvisala...
Ti maledice...
Aida Ah! no!...

9. "You are just the pharaohs' slave!" (lines 85–86). Two *quinari doppi* without rhyme for the *parola scenica*:[5]

Aida	Padre...
Amonasro	Va indegna! non sei mia prole[6]...
	Dei Faraoni tu sei la schiava!

10. Aida is doomed; she will do what her father requests, in order to rescue their country. Amonasro hides himself (lines 87–94). Two quatrains of *quinari doppi*, with the rhyme scheme *abbc dcec* (the rhyme *c* being a *rima tronca*):

Aida	Padre, a costoro schiava io non sono...
	Non maledirmi... non imprecarmi...
	Tua figlia ancora potrai chiamarmi...
	Della mia patria degna sarò!
Amonasro	Pensa che un popolo, vinto, straziato,
	Per te soltanto risorger può...
Aida	O patria! o patria... quanto mi costi!
Amonasro	Coraggio! ei giunge... là tutto udrò...

As a whole, then, the duet is articulated in three distinct parts, each of them characterized by its meter and rhyme scheme, in turn determined by their dramatic content and function. The two "bridges" in recitative style between the three parts do not function as links; they serve to emphasize the *parola scenica* and isolate it from the symmetry of the musical discourse. In any case, for dramatic purposes Verdi rejects in this duet the conventional organization in four parts that had been customary in Italian opera from the time of Rossini: Allegro, Cantabile, Allegro, and Cabaletta.[7] He does not hesitate to return to it, for instance, when the drama requires it in the scene immediately following, the Aida-Radamès duet.

The verbal structure, therefore, implies the musical structure in its points of articulation. The position of the set pieces, and their internal organization, are results of the overall conception of the musical drama; in giving binding instructions to Ghislanzoni, Verdi refuses or accepts, according to the needs of the drama, the conventions of nineteenth-century Italian opera. The duet has the form of an arch, whose culminating point coincides with the *parola scenica*: "Dei Faraoni tu sei la schiava!"; but its articulation can be understood only if considered in the economy of the entire act and of the opera as a whole. All this becomes even clearer if we compare the text of the libretto with the *programme*, or scenario written by Mariette Bey, which has only recently been published. The main difference between the two texts lies in the dramatic coherence (and resulting tension) given by Verdi to that succession of events, logically understandable but rather ineffective and poorly organized from a dramatic point of view:

The set represents a garden of the palace. On the left the oblique façade of a pavilion, or tent. At the back of the stage runs the Nile. On the horizon

> the Libyan mountains, vividly illuminated by the sunset. Statues, palm trees, tropical bushes. As the curtain rises, Aida is alone on stage. Radamès is in her thoughts and heart more than ever. The trees, the sacred river which runs at her feet, those distant hills—where the ancestors of her beloved rest—all this is witness of her constancy and fidelity. She is waiting for him. May Isis, protector of love, lead him to her, who wants to be only his. But it is not Radamès who comes, it is Amonasro. [Here follows a description of Amonasro's appearance.] He informs his daughter that Ethiopia has again lifted the flag of revolt, and that Radamès will again march against it. In a moving speech he reminds her of the land where she was born, of her desolated mother, of the sacred images of their ancestors' gods. But the love inspired by Aida in Radamès has not escaped his fatherly intuition (or premonition). She should take advantage of this love to seize from Radamès the secret plan for the Egyptian troops' march. Radamès will be taken during the battle, and led as a slave to Ethiopia, where eternal bonds will ensure forever their happiness. Won by her father's supplications, by the remembrance of her childhood, by the joy at the idea of being united to her beloved—away from a land where she has suffered all too long the tortures of slavery—Aida promises.[8]

If the dramatic structure and the verbal organization already contain the essence of the episode, what then is the function of music? In my opinion, it is twofold: not only does it characterize in its own terms the elements of the dramatic discourse but—and this is its crucial function—it determines its temporal dimension, its duration. These durations should not therefore be valued in abstract and absolute terms (indeed the same is true for the characterizing musical elements); on the contrary, they should be related to the other durations that determine episodes, scenes, acts, the entire opera.

By shifting from the purple light of the sunset, as in the *programme*, to the dark night of the libretto, Verdi created the possibility of characterizing the entire opening scene with the simplest of all "musico-dramatic signs"—to use the terminology of Frits Noske[9]—a simple note, G.[10] This pitch repeated at different octaves by the violins, and around which unfolds also the "exotic" melody entrusted to the flute, is further defined by the particular color the composer gives it by using the overtones in the divided cellos; the sonority of G is—so to speak—"wrapped" with these overtones, which give it an unmistakable character. This G is sustained in the orchestra throughout the chorus—offstage—of priests and priestesses, thirty-four bars altogether Andante mosso;[11] it is interrupted at the beginning of the dialogue between Amneris and Ramfis, and it starts again on the last sentence of the high priest, continuing further for fourteen bars, during which the material of the introductory chorus is repeated "telescoped," as is the melody entrusted to the flute.[12] Through this dovetailing of the sonority of G onto the recitative, and with the recapitulation of the opening material, the dramatic point is perfectly established, and Amneris and Ramfis are "absorbed" into the night, cold and impassive as is the chanting of the priests. All this is realized dramatically by Verdi not with musical gestures but with the very absence of them: the dramatic situation is defined by the static persistence of just one pitch.

Both the stage direction in the score and the *disposizione scenica* ask at this point for an "empty stage for a few moments,"[13] but Aida's arrival is announced by the motif that characterizes her throughout the opera, and her few sentences of recitative lead directly into the two-verse Romanza.[14] In contrast with Mariette Bey's *programme*, in which Aida, like a Metastasio heroine, calls on surrounding nature as witness of her fidelity to her beloved, the libretto emphasizes just one "affect," a desperate longing for her home country; and in the score all this is carried to the extreme. Verdi takes the last line of the first quatrain, "Oh patria mia, mai più ti rivedrò," and transforms it into a true *Leitmotif* of the Romanza. The melodically passionate declamation of this line is preceded by an instrumental "figure," entrusted to two oboes, two clarinets in C, and a flute, modally articulated, which concludes first on F (four bars) and then on E (six bars).[15] This modal contour and this instrumental color have an important structural function in the economy of the act; they return later, during the Aida-Radamès duet, when Aida mentions the "novella patria" to her beloved, her own country where they will take refuge.[16] The Romanza is articulated in two verses that are parallel also from a musical point of view; the second verse opens with the repetition of the *second* phrase (six bars long)[17] of the instrumental "figure," and it is varied, in comparison with the first verse, only in the figurations of the accompaniment and in its scoring, and it is three bars shorter; a small coda, a sort of cadenza, repeats the *Leitmotif*—both instrumental "figure" and melodic line[18]—thus sealing the dramtic function of the Romanza: it is only because of this longing for her home country that Amonasro can bend Aida to his will. The musical articulation of all the "signs" that characterize Aida's "affect," especially their duration, is determined by their dramatic function. It was necessary first to state them, and then to prolong them for sixty bars Andantino mosso. Only by being given a pertinent temporal dimension can they acquire the necessary weight in the economy of the drama.

The duet between Aida and Amonasro opens with a quick recitative, given almost exclusively to "that proud and cunning king," as Verdi puts it:[19] twenty-eight measures Allegro vivo, just to sketch the ancillary events, and then back *in medias res*.[20] The three stages through which Amonasro pushes his daughter into the trap prepared for her have in common the same metrical structure (eleven-syllable lines alternately *piani* and *tronchi*) as well as the same rhyme scheme. This tripartite articulation unified by common elements is perfectly matched at the musical level.[21] The musical meter is the same, 4/4, in the three sections, as is the key signature, five flats; but the relationship between these sections is a dynamic one, since the tension is gradually increased through the modification of common "signs":

1. a semiquaver ostinato in the violas (example 6.1) moves, altered, to the cellos in the second section (example 6.2) and finally, in the third section, is entrusted to the first violins (example 6.3).

EXAMPLE 6.1

EXAMPLE 6.2

EXAMPLE 6.3

2. the melodic phrase given to Amonasro (example 6.4), at the beginning relaxed and cantabile, is altered as shown in example 6.5, where the rhythm remains the same, but the melodic shape becomes tense and moves to the relative minor; in the third section the vocal part becomes a sort of declamation, dissociated from the movement in the orchestra (example 6.6).

EXAMPLE 6.4

Example 6.5

Example 6.6

3. the first section is in D♭ major, the second in the relative minor, B♭ minor, moving to B♭ major at the intervention of Aida; the third section again in B♭ minor;
4. the crescendo concerns the agogic as well, from Allegro giusto (MM. 100 to the quarter-note) in the first two sections to Poco più animato (MM. 116 to the quater-note) in the third section. Furthermore, the first section is seventeen bars long, the second twenty, the third only eight.

The musical crescendo is the direct result of the dramatic situation, the cruel trap into which Aida is led without her realizing it. It is important also to notice that each of these sections, from the point of view of the harmonic rhythm,[22] is very static at the beginning, while their second part is richer in changes of harmony. In other words, Verdi first states and then develops the "signs" of his dramatic language and clearly distinguishes between static and dynamic durations.[23] The last section, as we have seen, is by far the shortest and it is dovetailed with the recitative. Notice how the figuration in example 6.7 becomes the figure shown in example 6.8, punctuating the crescendo of Amonasro's insinuating questions. The gradual thinning of the texture in the orchestra points in the same direction, as does the sequence of the cellos' motif (example 6.9). Aida finally understands, refuses horrified, and Amonasro explodes.

Example 6.7

Example 6.8

Example 6.9

The central part of the duet is subdivided, as is the first part, into three sections, both at the verbal and at the musical level. As in the first part, each section is linked to the following by common musical features.[24] The meter, 6/8, is the same, and the three sections are connected by a harmonic relationship, though by no means a "classical" one: C minor, A♭ major, E minor. Actually, these keys are neither established nor developed through cadential or even tonal movements; rather than keys, they are better regarded as tonal levels, and indeed one follows the other without clear-cut cadential caesurae, and they are more and more unstable as the dramatic tension grows. Each of these sections is subdivided, as are the previous sections of the duet, into two parts: one part, in which the main musical "sign" is asserted,[25] is harmonically static; in the other the "sign" is elaborated and developed in musical terms.

The *parola scenica* central to the duet—"Non sei mia figlia! Dei Faraoni tu sei la schiava!" (example 6.10)—exploits the highest register of the baritone voice and, at the same time, almost completely dispenses with the orchestra. The contrast between elements of dynamics and of texture, on which the crescendo in dramatic tension is built up from the previous pages, reaches at this culminating point its extreme and most elementary form. The dramatic climax coincides with the barest use of language.

The third part of the duet, Andante assai sostenuto (MM. 76 to the quarter-note), lasts thirty-one bars and is identified and unified, as are the previous parts, by common musical "signs": first of all by the rhythmic pedal in the violins, which is extended through its entire duration, a musical transfiguration of Aida's inner sighing. This part is also in one key only, D♭ major, the key of the opening section of the duet. Here also a first section, characterized by the repetition of the rhythmic pedal on the dominant—A♭—and corresponding to Aida's broken utterances *molto sotto voce e cupo*,[26] is followed by its dynamic counterpart, in which the syncopated pedal moves, always in the violins, upward stepwise for the span of no less than two octaves, and where the harmonic rhythm undergoes different subtle fluctuations. Considering the first bar as introductory, the borderline between the two sections of this part of the duet is placed exactly halfway through, that is at the sixteenth bar, in correspondence with the beginning of the second quatrain of *quinari doppi* and, dramatically, with Amonasro's hypocritical "consoling" intervention.

A more detailed and thorough analysis would certainly reveal other symmetries and relationships between the various components of the musico-dramatic

Example 6.10

language of this episode. On the basis of what has been said about this one example, I would like now to identify some of the general principles that govern the unfolding of the dramatic "language" of opera. They can be summarized as follows:

1. The articulation of the musical language is already present in the organization of the libretto. In other words, the verbal structure is determined by the musical structure and is governed by dramatic principles. From this follows that every analysis on the purely musical level of an opera score is bound to be incomplete and in the end to fail in its essential purpose; such an analysis grasps only one aspect of the musico-dramatic language and constantly risks missing the essential point.
2. All the elements of the musical language can be used as "signs"; they may be articulated as "themes," and have a complex organization defined by key, rhythm, melodic shape, harmony, timbre. They may, however, be just sonorities, or simple pitches used per se, without articulation, and yet be by no means less effective dramatically. Indeed, the simpler the musical "sign," the more complex and articulated its dramatic function.

3. The articulation of these musical "signs" is directly related to their duration, that is, to their temporal dimension. A "sign" that is not characterized by an appropriate duration becomes unrecognizable and ceases to be a "sign."
4. The articulation of a musical "sign" can be static; the "sign" is sustained, or repeated without modification throughout its duration. But it can also have a dynamic temporal dimension, during which it is developed, modified, and related to other "signs," albeit always recognizable in its identity. One can find also both static and dynamic articulations of the same "sign"—static articulations to assert it, dynamic articulations to qualify its function during its temporal dimension.
5. The value and the function of a musico-dramatic "sign" can in no way be evaluated in abstract, by taking the "sign" in isolation as an absolute musical element. Instead, one must always take into consideration its position, its articulation through well-defined durations, not only within the episode in which it appears but also—and especially—as a part of a larger dramatic structure, as a structural factor in a scene, in an act, as a constituent element of the entire opera.

Notes

1. The original Italian text of the libretto is available, besides the current Ricordi edition, in Luigi Baldacci, ed., *Tutti i libretti di Verdi* (Milan, 1975), 449–71. For the present study, however, I follow the libretto printed for the first Italian performance: *Aida.* Opera in quattro atti. Versi di A. Ghislanzoni. Musica di G. Verdi. R. Teatro alla Scala. Carnevale-Quaresima 1871–72 (Milan, Naples, and Rome, 1872). The layout of the print in this edition clearly reveals the poetic structure. The edition also contains some very interesting variants from the text as it appears in the score. I will indicate these variants in the corresponding places. For an English translation of the Italian libretto, see W. Weaver, *Seven Verdi Librettos . . . with the Original Italian* (New York, 1975), 343–415.

2. The known Verdi-Ghislanzoni correspondence is published in G. Cesari and A. Luzio, eds., *I copialettere di Giuseppe Verdi* (Milan, 1913), 635–75. A few of the letters have been published in English translation in E. Istel, "A genetic study of the *Aida* libretto," *The Musical Quarterly* 3 (1917): 34–52; and in Charles Osborne, ed., *Letters of Giuseppe Verdi* (London, 1972), 155–67. The most comprehensive collection of documents concerning the birth of *Aida* and its early years is H. Busch, ed., *Verdi's "Aida"—The History of an Opera in Letters and Documents* (Minneapolis, 1978). It is, however, absolutely essential to consult also Philip Gossett, "Verdi, Ghislanzoni, and *Aida*: The Uses of Conventions," *Critical Inquiry* I (1974): 291–334: in this important essay not only is a correct chronology of the extant correspondence established but also basic compositional conventions—especially for the duets—are identified; these conventions determine the overall as well as the detailed structure of the libretto, and they are typical of nineteenth-century Italian opera. For Aida's Romanza, see the letter of Verdi to Ghislanzoni of 5 August 1871 (*Copialettere*, 674–75: Busch, *Verdi's "Aida,"* 196–97; Istel, "A Genetic Study," 47).

3. For a detailed analysis of the Italian metrical organization as applied to opera, see R. A. Moreen, *Integration of Text Forms and Musical Forms in Verdi's Early Operas* (Ann Arbor and London, 1979), and J. Budden, *The Operas of Verdi*, vol. 2 (London, 1978), 17ff.

4. In the score: "gioia."

5. With this term Verdi indicates "the word that cuts (*scolpisce*) the dramatic situation and makes it clear and evident": letter to Ghislanzoni of 17 August 1870; see *Copialettere*, 641; Osborne, *Letters of Verdi*, 159 (a pale and imprecise translation). Busch, *Verdi's "Aida,"* 50, gives another translation. The above is mine.

6. In the score, Verdi destroys the metrical structure by changing the line into a much more direct and effective "Non sei mia figlia!" (You are not my daughter).

7. See Gossett, "Verdi, Ghislanzoni," 300–306.

8. J. Humbert, "A propos de l'égyptomanie dans l'oeuvre de Verdi: attribution à Auguste Mariette d'un scénario anonyme de l'opéra *Aida*," *Revue de Musicologie* 62 (1976): 229–56. The passage quoted here is on pp. 250–51 (text in French and in Italian; the translation is mine).

9. Frits Noske, *The Signifier and the Signified—Studies in the Operas of Mozart and Verdi* (The Hague, 1977; reprint, Oxford, 1990); this book is a landmark in research on musical drama; it is the first attempt to apply systematically the principles of semiotics to the problems of opera, seen as the meeting point of different systems of communication. Particularly important, from a methodological point of view, is appendix 1, "Semiotic Devices in Musical Drama," 309–21, from which I take the following definition: "*Musico-dramatic sign* . . .—A musical unit which stresses, clarifies, invalidates, contradicts or supplies an element of the libretto. The sign is semantically interpretable and discloses dramatic truth" (316).

10. On the dramatic function of single sonorities in Verdi's operas, see also chap. 5 of the present volume.

11. Giuseppe Verdi, *Aida*. Opera in quattro atti. Libretto di A. Ghislanzoni. Partitura d'orchestra [Milan], G. Ricordi, s.a., pl. no. P.R. 153, 265–67. The reader is kindly urged to consult the orchestral score while reading the following pages.

12. Ibid., 269–70.

13. Ibid., 271; Giulio Ricordi, *Disposizione scenica per l'opera "Aida."* Versi di A. Ghislanzoni. Musica di G. Verdi, compilata e regolata secondo la messa in scena del Teatro alla Scala da G. R. [Milan, Naples, Rome], G. Ricordi, s.a., pl. no. 43504, 40.

14. Verdi calls Aida's solo a Romanza (and not an Aria), no doubt because of the basically strophic nature of the piece, as opposed to the structure of a regular aria, where a Cantabile is followed by a Cabaletta. On the use of the term Romanza in Verdi's operas, see Martin Chusid, "The Organization of Scenes with Arias: Verdi's Cavatinas and Romanzas," *Atti del I° congresso internazionale di studi verdiani* (Parma, 1969) 59–66, especially 61–62 and 66.

15. Orchestral score, 273.

16. Ibid., 316–17.

17. Ibid., 275, last system.

18. Ibid., 278, second system.

19. Letter to Ghislanzoni of 7 October [1870]. See *Copialettere*, 650; Busch, *Verdi's "Aida,"* 75.

20. Orchestral score, 279–80.

21. In the orchestral score the first section (Allegro giusto, MM. 100 to the quarter-note, rehearsal letter I) spans from the beginning of p. 281 to the penultimate bar of the second system, p. 283; the second section, starting from this bar, ends on the first chord of p. 288 (rehearsal letter J); finally, the third section (Poco più animato, MM. 116 to the quarter-note) runs up to the third bar in the first system of p. 289, but the musical flow continues without break in the ensuing recitative.

22. This term commonly signifies the rhythm created in a musical composition by changes in the harmony.

23. For instance, the static dimension is created by the absence of harmonic rhythm, emphasized by an A♭ pedal distributed among three instruments: oboe (top A♭ held for seven and half bars), violas, which repeat the figuration of example 6.1, and the basses (cellos and double basses), which repeat the pitch (at different octave levels) on the rhythm ♫♩♬♩♫♩♬♩♪ .

24. The first section (Allegro, dotted quarter-note 96, rehearsal letter K) goes from p. 292 to the first bar of p. 296; the second from this bar to the first bar of p. 298 (rehearsal letter L); the third section from this bar to the last bar of p. 300; as in the first part of the duet, there is no break with the following recitative.

25. Here again the static dimension is realized above all by the absence of harmonic rhythm: in the first section, by the persistence (six bars) of the C-minor chord; in the third, by the pedal on top B in the first violins (ten bars).

26. The extraordinary expressive power of this page, one of the greatest and most moving moments in Verdi's music, derives from the contrast between the ostinato pedal in the violins and the melody entrusted to the violas, cellos, and one bassoon, playing in unison ***ppp*** *con espressione*. This melody is articulated, both in detail and at the overall level, following the principles of the poetic quatrain in nineteenth-century Italian opera, in consequence of which the first and second lines have the function of asserting a situation, the third of developing the tension to its maximum, and the fourth of concluding the episode (see the Dallapiccola essay on the subject, already cited in chap. 1, n. 31). In the melody we are considering, the poetic line has its equivalent in a melodic fragment one bar long, the quatrain in a four-bar phrase. Significantly, Aida sings in unison with this melody only from the beginning of the third quatrain ("Ancor tua figlia . . . "), and the climax of the episode—corresponding with the highest pitch of the melodic line—lies in the second "line" of the fourth "quatrain," at the words "della *mia* patria."

CHAPTER 7

MORE ON THE THREE "SYSTEMS": THE FIRST ACT OF *LA FORZA DEL DESTINO*

IN MUSICAL theater, three "systems" of communication act simultaneously, each operating in accordance with its own nature and laws. Their combination, however, is something more than their sum total or simple juxtaposition. These "systems" are:

1. *the dramatic action*, in which the events on stage unfold;
2. *the verbal organization* of the dialogue, which embodies the interaction between characters onstage and is in most cases structured in lines and verses; and
3. *the music*, by which I mean not merely the singing of the poetic text but also the instrumental part(s) that move with it. The function of the music is twofold: it establishes the temporal dimension of the dramatic events, and it characterizes them through its own means.

An analysis of the interaction of these three "systems" can reveal a great deal about the nature of a musico-dramatic event; and such analysis may also have a historical dimension, since it may help place the piece in the context of the author's total output and within the history of its time.[1]

I have always been fascinated by the dramatic power of the first act of *La forza del destino*, and my curiosity about its effectiveness led me to the remarks that follow. Debatable though they may be, they will perhaps shed some light on the opera's true dramatic content and its position within Verdi's opus.[2]

Julian Budden summarizes the action of *La forza del destino*, Act I, as follows:

> SEVILLE. In a room in their shabby villa on the outskirts of the city, the marquis of Calatrava is bidding his daughter a fond goodnight. But Leonora is deeply unhappy and remorseful, since she has resolved that very night to elope with Don Alvaro. In a Romanza [. . .] she expresses her

The ideas and conclusions contained in this chapter were first presented in April 1980 during the Sixth International Verdi Conference, organized and sponsored by the University of California at Irvine.

> sorrow at leaving home forever. Her maid Curra, however, is only too anxious to be gone. The sound of galloping hooves is heard, and Don Alvaro enters through the French windows and plunges into a duet with Leonora [. . .]; but soon he notices with dismay that Leonora is reluctant to leave with him; she begs him to wait just one more day. Sadly he prepares to abandon all thought of their elopement, when Leonora has a sudden change of heart. Their Cabaletta of joy [. . .] is cut short by a commotion outside. The marquis enters followed by his servants, whom he orders to arrest the "vile seducer." But Alvaro will surrender only to the marquis himself. He throws down his pistol, which accidentally fires; the marquis falls, mortally wounded, and curses his daughter with his last breath.[3]

The dramatic action thus unfolds in four stages: a dialogue between Leonora and her father; Leonora's monologue; the arrival of Don Alvaro and their unsuccessful attempt at elopement; and, finally, the accidental death of the marquis. These events are linked by a common element: Leonora's ambivalent feelings. She is torn between respectful affection for her father and passionate love for Don Alvaro; throughout the act she is at the center of the action. Her ambivalence gives different dramatic meaning to each of the four sections: the first shows her relationship to her father; the second illustrates the inner conflict that torments her soul; the third explores her relationship with Don Alvaro; and in the fourth episode an external, fortuitous event sets in motion the tragic development of Leonora's life from the premises established in the previous sections. There is a clear increase in dramatic tension during the unfolding of these four moments: from an almost "everyday" scene at the beginning to a highly dramatic (not to mention highly improbable) situation at the end. These four moments were, of course, identified, distinguished from one another, characterized, and articulated at the verbal level, in the libretto. Francesco Maria Piave fashioned the opening scene, the dialogue between the marquis and his daughter, in the most conventional recitative meter, *versi sciolti* or eleven- and seven-syllable lines freely alternated. But a musical setting in plain recitative style would have prevented the dialogue from assuming any dramatic relevance. In order to make the scene properly significant, Verdi "invented" a short musical number, one whose articulation rests entirely with the orchestra and which is built on the "exposition," "development," and "recapitulation" of a simple musical idea, two measures long (example 7.1).[4]

Verdi called this "number" "Introduzione-scena," a type of musical organization that he was to use at least twice more and, significantly, in both cases in exactly the same dramatic position: the very beginning of the action. An Introduzione-scena opens *Aida* with a dialogue between Ramfis and Radamès;[5] and it does so again—developed in a temporal framework much larger than that of these two earlier operas—in the revised (1881) version of *Simon Boccanegra*.[6] The

EXAMPLE 7.1

Aida "number" follows very closely the pattern established in *La forza del destino*: both pieces move at a "two-measure" pace; both are rather short and firmly set in a single key (E major in *Forza*; G major in *Aida*), with a central episode (the "development") of four measures that is a third apart from the main key (G major in *Forza*; B major in *Aida*); finally, they are both followed by a Romanza. Through this type of musical organization an otherwise neutral dialogue becomes dramatically relevant but without any emphasis being placed on the characters involved. Rather, through the "Introduzione-scena" Verdi presents one or more of the dramatic elements from which the action will develop—in the case of *La forza del destino*, Leonora's relationship with her father and with the world from which she comes.

Toward the end of the episode a sudden harmonic shift (to E♭ major!) contradicts for a moment the tonal stability.[7] The shift occurs at Leonora's outburst "Oh, padre mio!" (example 7.2) and reveals her true emotional state. It is all the more powerful in that it contrasts with the tonal balance of the previous measures. A short dialogue between Leonora and Curra in secco recitative style, almost entirely without orchestral accompaniment, leads to Leonora's Romanza, which is articulated in three quatrains of *settenari*:

EXAMPLE 7.2

Me pellegrina ed orfana
Lungi dal patrio nido
Un fato inesorabile
Sospinge a stranio lido...

Colmo di tristi immagini
Da' suoi rimorsi affranto
E' il cor di questa misera
Dannato a eterno pianto...

Ti lascio, ohimé, con lacrime
Dolce mia terra!... addio.
Ahimé, non avrà termine
Sì gran dolore!... Addio.

[A wandering orphan,
Far from my secure homeland,
An inexorable fate
Pushes me to strange shores...

Weighed down with sad visions
Of his troubled remorse,
The heart of this miserable one
Condemned to eternal tears...

I leave you, alas, with tears,
My sweet homeland!... adieu.
Alas, such great sorrow
Will have no end!... Adieu.]

It has often been stated that this text was transferred word-for-word from Somma's libretto for *King Lear.*[8] In fact, there are significant metrical and textual variants between the *Forza* version and Cordelia's farewell to her father's court.[9] Somma's text consists of four stanzas, the first two a sestet and a quatrain of *settenari*, the last two both quatrains of *ottonari*. This structure powerfully supports Budden's theory that even if the poetic text was imitated in *La forza del destino* the music was not, because of the differing position and function of the musical "numbers" within the two operas. Rather than a Romanza, Somma's text suggests a full-scale aria, one with a concluding Cabaletta. Piave's three quatrains paraphrase Somma's first two, using in addition their alternation of *sdruccioli* and *piani*, and some of their rhymes. But, as we see from Somma's first two stanzas, the differences are at least as great as the similarities:

Me pellegrina ed orfana
Lunge dal ciel natio

Preme il destino mio.
E a' flutti inesorabili
Piena di sue memorie
Fra' i miei dolor m'avvìo!

Non ho per te che lacrime
Dolce Inghilterra, addìo.
Senza immortale angoscia
Non ti si perde... addìo.

[A wandering orphan
Far from my homeland's skies,
This is what fate has forced on me.
And with inexorable waves
Full of its memories
I set off with my sorrow!

I have only tears for you
Sweet England, adieu.
I will not leave you
Without everlasting anguish... adieu.]

The difference in metrical structure, and consequently in musical setting—a Romanza as opposed to an aria with Cabaletta—is justified by the position of each set-piece. As Budden writes: "In Somma's drama it was to have been an aria for Cordelia after she has been disinherited and driven out by her father, and it would conclude the first scene of the opera. Therefore the musical setting would have had a 'conclusive' structure at least as marked as, say, 'Ritorna vincitor.'"[10] But at this point in his stylistic development, instead of a set-piece consisting of two strongly contrasting sections, Verdi preferred a "number" in which a single "affect" was presented and developed within a suitable duration; a "number" thus structured would be much more easily integrated into the overall structure of the act. Above all, Verdi wanted to give Leonora's inner conflict an appropriate temporal dimension—something to which the Romanza structure was perfectly suited.

It will be useful here to cite Martin Chusid's definition of the Romanza:

> Verdi's *romanzas* [. . .] are written more often for the tenor than for the soprano and they may occur anywhere in the opera [. . .]. Their texts are usually more serious than those of *cavatinas*, a fact which may explain why the larger number of *romanzas* make important use of the minor mode (i.e. nine of the thirteen listed in Appendix II). Eight of these nine *romanzas* in minor are designed to conclude in major. As a result, Verdi provides for many of them a bipartite frame—the first part in minor, the second in

major. See, for example, Leonora's "Me pellegrina ed orfana" from the first act of *La forza del destino*.[11]

Verdi maintains this bipartite structure even when the text is articulated in three stanzas: the points of articulation coincide with those of the poetic text, but each section has a different duration. In the present case, the entire Romanza moves in a series of eight-measure phrases, each section comprising the simple declamation (or the repetition) of a stanza. But within this uniformity, the differences are striking. In the first eight measures the opening quatrain is declaimed; the second quatrain occupies twice as much time as the first, its structure neatly divided into eight plus eight measures (in the second eight the text is repeated); the third quatrain, however, takes as much time as the two previous ones put together:

stanza 1	stanza 2	stanza 3	coda and cadenza
8 mm.	8 + 8 mm.	8 + 8 + 8 mm.	5 mm.
------minor---------------		---------major------------	

The expansion within each section is achieved mostly through dominant pedal points, a device that coincides in the vocal part with the sequential expansion of melodic cells. "Me pellegrina ed orfana" is, then, bipartite in more than one sense: not only in its progression from a section in minor to one in major but also in the different time span allotted to the declamation of the stanzas of poetic text, the first two stanzas taking as much time as does the third alone. Furthermore, the temporal bipartition determined by the structure of the poetic text does *not* coincide with that marked by the change of mode, in that the section in major starts eight measures *after* the beginning of the second part of the Romanza (see the preceding diagram). The caesura between the two parts is clearly marked by a general pause, followed in the orchestral score by a double bar and the indication "Tempo I." This kind of bipartite structure, in addition to the alternation of mode, is already present at a lower structural level. Each eight-measure section in fact moves at a two-measure pace and already alternates between major and minor. It is precisely because of this complex and yet clearly discernible organization that Leonora's ambivalent feelings are communicated to us so directly. The constant modal ambivalence and the structural contrast of sections mirror (or rather depict) the contrast that torments her soul.

A second, short dialogue between Leonora and Curra, again almost lacking in orchestral accompaniment (if we exclude the onomatopoeic rendering of the horses' arrival), leads directly to the duet with Don Alvaro. It is clear that, at least in this act, Verdi aimed at developing the musico-dramatic discourse almost exclusively through set-pieces, with recitative passages merely supplying a connective function.

The general formal pattern of the duet adheres very closely to that outlined by Philip Gossett:[12] an Allegro *tempo d'attacco* is followed by a section in slower tempo, differing in both key and meter; a faster *tempo di mezzo* (again with a change in tonality and meter) leads to a final section, the Cabaletta. I should stress that this four-part structure is clear already at the verbal level, each of the parts being characterized by a different poetic meter and rhyme scheme. The introductory Allegro in E♭ (MM. 138 to the quarter-note) is built on four quatrains of *ottonari*. The first, given entirely to Don Alvaro, depicts his generous, ardent nature; the vocal line carries the entire weight of the section and follows the structure of the poetic text in that each melodic phrase corresponds exactly to a line of the quatrain. But with the second quatrain the articulation shifts to the orchestra: Leonora's tormented emotions are characterized by a rhythmic pattern that Verdi had already exploited successfully in the first section of the Act I trio in *Il trovatore* (a passage also depicting anguish and suspense).[13] Verdi singles out the third quatrain with appropriate musical means. I have already mentioned Luigi Dallapiccola's pioneering essay "Words and Music in Italian Opera"[14] and his views on the importance of this quatrain in the four-verse structure as an organization typical of the Italian operatic and vocal tradition. "The drama takes place in the third verse," wrote Dallapiccola, meaning that its phrase structure, metrical pulse, rhythmic organization, and melodic and harmonic pace are in sharp contrast to those of the two preceding quatrains, where the basic "affect" had been established. The third quatrain in the opening section of the first duet in *La forza del destino* singles out one of the basic elements of the entire opera: Alvaro's love for Leonora ("Ma d'amor sì puro e santo / nulla opporsi può all'incanto"), here stated for the first time. Preceded by a three-beat rest, this quatrain's setting is thrown in the strongest relief by a sudden shift from the dominant minor of E♭ (B♭ minor) to G♭. It is in slower tempo (MM. 120 to the quarter-note, instead of 138) and larger temporal values, and its obvious melodic character is underlined by the indication "cantabile." The quatrain, in turn, is organized according to the same principles that govern its larger structural level: its third line ("E Dio stesso il nostro palpito") coincides with a marked increase in harmonic rhythm and with the stepwise descent of the bass line, which reaches the strongest point of tension (V^7 with the seventh in the bass) at the same time as the highest pitch in the vocal line (A♭). This melodic phrase, which identifies Alvaro's love for Leonora, is presented here for the first time in the opera. But the idea, as David Lawton has shown, has a rich future history and therefore larger structural function. It returns three times more in the score: in the instrumental episode—the clarinet solo—at the beginning of the third act; in the recitativelike measures immediately thereafter that introduce Don Alvaro's Romanza, "Oh tu che in seno agli angeli"; and finally in the seventh scene of the third act, again in the orchestra, in the introduction to the duet between Don Alvaro and Don Carlo. In its instrumental version, the melodic idea is always entrusted to the clarinet; but, even more significantly, its series of statements is arranged in progressively descending tonal sequence (G♭, F, E minor), becoming at the same time shorter and shorter.[15] We have here a procedure typical of Verdi's dramaturgy: while apparently respectful—or at least making use of—traditional principles of organization (in this case the standard duet pattern), the composer identified, *inside these structures and without contradicting them*, thematic cells and musical idioms that have a function in the overall structure of the opera. In discussing this kind of material, Joseph Kerman has drawn a neat distinction between "recalling themes" and "identifying themes"[16] and has clearly shown their traditional derivation: "Identifying themes are sung or played when the group, person, or idea is strongly in evidence, like a sonorous or 'hermeneutic' extension of its physical or psychological presence. They are not used to link one stage of the drama to another, but simply to identify or make vivid. They serve to remind the audience rather than to remind the people in the play."[17] It seems to me that Don Alvaro's theme, while certainly identifying him (or, more precisely, identifying his love for Leonora), was used by Verdi with a specific, unequivocally structural function in the organization of the whole opera. "Identifying themes" most certainly are not *Leitmotiven* in the Wagnerian sense (as is obviously implied by Kerman, when he asserts that they do not "link one stage of the drama to another"), but the way in which they are presented certainly helps to connect and relate various moments of the opera.

To return to the duet between Leonora and Don Alvaro, the fourth quatrain of the opening Allegro resumes the type of organization already seen in the second. The articulation is once again in the orchestra rather than the vocal parts, and the declamation is again broken: once more, Leonora's distress is at the forefront. The first section of the duet, however, is markedly different from a traditional setting in that any sense of conclusion is carefully avoided. Instead, the suspense is further enhanced by harmonic means. The series of keys through which the four quatrains move are:

First quatrain: E♭ major
Second quatrain: E♭ minor
Third quatrain: G♭ major to D♭ major
Fourth quatrain: F minor, ending on F (without the third!)

Since the second large section of the duet is in B♭ major, the last quatrain functions as a kind of dominant preparation. In this way, a direct musical link, and a very strong sense of continuity between the two sections, is firmly established.

In the libretto, the second section of the duet is made up of six quatrains of *quinari doppi*, which extend to Alvaro's exclamation "Eleonora!" However, only the first two quatrains are set in a tempo, meter, and key that correspond to a traditional second section: the 3/8 Andantino (MM. 92 to the eighth-note) in B♭

major. In these two quatrains (in which the articulation is entirely given over to the vocal line, and melodic phrase length and poetic line structure exactly correspond) Alvaro—still unaware of Leonora's anguish—announces that their union will be blessed at the rising of the sun. But Leonora is far from ready to follow him: the *tempo di mezzo* abruptly begins as she again enters the dialogue, with a sudden shift to common time and Allegro agitato (MM. 144 to the quarter-note), although with no change of key. Once again, continuity is of paramount importance at this point in the action and prevails over the established convention set out by the libretto's metrical organization. So much so that this third section of the duet begins with a sort of dialogue in *recitativo accompagnato* style; only when Leonora tries in broken, sighing phrases to convince Alvaro of her "happiness" in following him does Verdi resume any kind of structured articulation.[18] The entire passage, starting from Leonora's "Anco una volta," was rewritten in the 1869 version of the opera.[19] However, what remains intact in both versions is the relationship of the voice and orchestra: in the St. Petersburg version, Leonora's utterances correspond in phrase length to the poetic text and are first echoed—then doubled in unison and at the octave—by similar phrases in the orchestra. In the 1869 version, while maintaining in the vocal line the kind of declamation in which the phrase lengths agree with the verbal structure, Verdi recalled in the orchestra a syncopated figure that had dominated the last duet in the final act of *Don Carlos* and used it as a rhythmic pedal for a good part of the episode.[20]

Seen from the dramatic point of view, the broken and irregular articulation of this *tempo di mezzo* is a necessity: at this point in the action there is strong contrast rather than agreement between the two characters. More than this: the entire section is a sort of preparation, a building up toward a climax that erupts in the utterance of a *parola scenica*. When Alvaro, finally aware of Leonora's inner torment and conflicts, declares solemnly that he is ready to renounce her and release her from all commitment, his beloved bursts out: "Son tua, son tua, tua col core e colla vita!" (I am yours, I am yours, with my heart and with my life!) This *parola scenica*, emphasized as so often in Verdi by a second-inversion chord (in this case D♭ major),[21] highlights the sudden change and leads directly to the final section of the duet, a Cabaletta *a due* in G♭ major—the key whose dominant was so strongly emphasized by the *parola scenica*. In *Aida*, Verdi was to return to this structural organization, undoubtedly prompted by the similarity of dramatic situation: in the central Allegro moderato of the third-act duet between Aida and Amonasro, any kind of tonal stability, and especially any sense of coherent harmonic movement, is carefully and purposefully avoided in order to reach the *parola scenica*: "Non sei mia figlia; dei Faraoni tu sei la schiava!" (You are not my daughter; you are the slave of the pharaohs!).[22] Here again the *parola scenica* is emphasized by a dominant (seventh) chord of the following section's tonality (A♭ and D♭ respectively).

The fourth and final part of the Leonora-Alvaro duet is built on two eight-line stanzas of *settenari*, the conventional Cabaletta meter: the first is for Leonora, the second for Alvaro, both characters expressing the same feeling of happiness at their forthcoming elopement. The melodic articulation of this section is entirely entrusted to the voices and is strictly modeled on the metrical organization of the text: each four-measure phrase corresponds to two poetic lines, and so each eight-line stanza follows precisely the "quatrain" principle described by Dallapiccola. The "squareness," the regular and simple articulation of the melodic movement, is powerfully enhanced by the harmony, in which the alternation of functional chords underlines the metrical structure of the text. To emphasize further the complete agreement of the two lovers, Alvaro literally repeats (to his own words) the sixteen measures just sung by Leonora.[23] The third part of the Cabaletta, in which the two voices exchange short phrases—introduced by Leonora and completed by Alvaro—is also sixteen measures long.

At this point, a conventional ending would bring back the melodic material of the Cabaletta's opening and introduce a strong cadential gesture, top notes for the voices, and elicit frenetic applause from the audience. But this would have destroyed the dramatic tension built in the previous scenes. The two voices join for four measures to sing, in strict imitation, the melodic phrase that first occurred at the close of the first part of the Cabaletta (lines 7–8 of Leonora's stanza); but suddenly footsteps are heard from within; the canonic movement and its orchestral accompaniment are abruptly halted. Verdi took the opening lines of the ensuing recitative ("Ascendono le scale," "Partiam," etc.) and grafted it onto the duet: the three onstage characters (Leonora, Curra, and Alvaro) express their reactions to the offstage noise over a dominant pedal on the timpani. The conventional organization is broken *from the inside*, a procedure that Verdi had successfully adopted since the time of *Rigoletto*.[24] In this way, the audience's attention is focused on the events onstage rather than on the soloists' vocal display. A last outburst of the concluding melody of the Cabaletta's first section—the only time in the entire duet in which the two voices sing in unison!—deceives no one: the cadence on G♭ is abruptly broken by the resumption of recitative (on a pedal a whole tone lower—from G♭ to E!), and the action leads directly to the "Scena-Finale I°."[25]

The last scene of the act is the most intriguing. In it, Verdi had to present in musical terms the events from which the tragedy unfolds in the subsequent acts. All the libretto offers are fourteen lines of *settenari doppi*, a meter generally adopted at moments of unusual dramatic importance (such as Azucena's "Condotta ell'era in ceppi," from the second act of *Il trovatore*), though it can also be found at culminating points in the dramatic action, with a function similar to that of the lines in *La forza del destino* now under examination. It is the meter of the gambling scene at the end of *La traviata*, Act II, of the whispering of the "congiurati" and of the last, desperate exchange between the lovers in the final scene of *Un ballo in maschera. Settenario doppio* is an extremely flexible meter, very close to the *versi sciolti* traditionally used in recitative. It is hardly accidental that all the examples just mentioned are rich in dramatic tension: they represent key points in the development of the plot rather than moments in which relaxed and peaceful "affects" and emotions can be expressed. In such scenes the meter allows the poet to give formal coherence to a text rich in action and movement, and in particular one "directional" in nature. In this way, the meter, by its mere presence, creates a specific dramatic entity in the libretto. Verdi took the fourteen lines as a whole and disregarded their inner organization almost entirely. Once again, as in the opening scene of the act, the musical articulation is entrusted entirely to the orchestra. And, to enhance further the inner coherence of this dramatic section, the composer turned to an organizing principle typical of the instrumental tradition—that of sonata form. The "first theme," in C♯ minor and eight measures long, is also a "recurring theme" in that it is constantly associated in the opera with Leonora's destiny.[26] It is presented first, as if to impress it most clearly on the audience, by the orchestra alone, at a dynamic level of ***ff*** and with a clear cadence in the tonic. It is then repeated, ***p***, accompanying the dialogue onstage, and now ends with a cadence on the dominant. Here the "second theme," in G♯ minor, is heard, its broad melodic character in sharp contrast to the "first theme." This "second theme," which makes use of internal repetition, lasts sixteen measures. What one might call the "development section" begins with twelve measures in which a brief melodic cell (example 7.3) is articulated contrapuntally and harmonically (example 7.4). This cell is powerfully reminiscent—it is in fact nothing more than an abbreviation—of the "first theme."

EXAMPLE 7.3

EXAMPLE 7.4

The second part of the "development" brings back the entire material of the exposition, but with a significant variant: the material is stated a tone lower, a procedure that—throughout Verdi's works but especially in this opera—has precise dramatic implications: the "first theme" is, as I have already said, constantly associated with Leonora, and its transposition a tone lower powerfully foreshadows her downfall. But the transposition also has a purely musical function: in presenting the "second theme" in F♯ minor, Verdi introduces the subdominant of the main key, C♯ minor, a key to which—after fifteen measures of modulation, and after the recurrence of the "second theme" on its dominant, G♯—the piece returns, with a perfect rounding-off of both theme and key. The return to the opening key, emphasized by the declamation of the tenor on the tonic pitch ("Eccomi inerme"), coincides with the accidental firing of the pistol that mortally wounds Leonora's father.

A short coda on an A-minor pedal, built on the melodic cell of example 8.4, creates enough tension to bring down the dying marquis's curse on Leonora (on a diminished-seventh chord, needless to say!), and the scene ends with a final return of the "first theme."

The organization of this "Scena-Finale I°" is certainly extraordinary in Italian opera; it is more striking still if one considers its temporal structure, both internally and in relation to the opening scene of the act. In spite of the "instrumental" organization adopted by Verdi for this episode, key words—almost the equivalent of *parole sceniche* when inserted in such a musical context—occur at structurally significant moments. The entire "Scena-Finale I°" consists of 8 measures of recitative *da dirsi presto* at the beginning and 165 measures of Allegro agitato e prestissimo (MM. 96 to the dotted quarter-note); the noble and dignified plea of Don Alvaro, "Signor di Calatrava," declaimed on F♯ without orchestral accompaniment and followed by an entire measure's rest, occurs at mm. 77–83—the very center of the episode, a sort of pivot point.

But even more impressive is the relationship of this last part of the act to the opening scene. The "Introduzione-scena" lasts forty-four measures, in Allegro moderato assai tempo, and with the metronome indication 96 to the dotted quarter-note. This means that the temporal ratio of these opening and concluding scenes is 1:4, or, in other words, that four measures of the concluding episode equal one measure of the initial scene. If we take the eight recitative measures *da dirsi presto* as equal in value to eight measures of the ensuing Allegro agitato e prestissimo, we can see that the two episodes have a duration that is almost identical. In this way, a perfect balance is built between the episodes that are pivotal to the entire act.

AT THE TIME of writing *La forza del destino*, Verdi had adopted a stance that was different from that of all other Italian composers of his time—not only through the various contacts and experiences that had enriched and enlarged his dramatic vocabulary in the preceding decade (in particular, of course, the Parisian experiences while writing *Les Vêpres siciliennes* and afterward) but especially through his extremely flexible use of compositional conventions deriving from the national tradition—above all those concerned with the relation of music to the metrical organization of the verbal text. From this point of view, what he acquired during the composition of *La forza del destino* was to bear its ripest fruits not immediately but a decade later, at the time of *Aida*, and perhaps even later still.

Far from being a linear, steady itinerary, Verdi's artistic development follows a tortuous, intermittent path. Only by verifying its truest structural articulation—and here the idea of the three "systems" proves extremely useful—can we assess and evaluate the connections among its various stages.

Notes

1. For a more detailed investigation of the interaction among these three "systems," see chapter 6, 113–26.

2. For a clearer understanding of what follows, the reader should have at hand the current Ricordi vocal score of the opera: Giuseppe Verdi, *La forza del destino* . . . Riduzione per canto e pianoforte di Luigi Truzzi. A cura di Mario Parenti (Milan, 1963), pl. no. 41381.

3. From the synopsis printed in the booklet accompanying the Deutsche Grammophon recording of *La forza del destino*, conducted by Giuseppe Sinopoli (1987).

4. See p. 13 of the vocal score cited in n.3. Julian Budden hears the bass line of this phrase as a variant of Leonora's prayer in Act II, "Deh, non m'abbandonar." See Julian Budden, *The Operas of Verdi*, vol. 2 (London, 1978), 448.

5. Giuseppe Verdi, *Aida* . . . Opera completa per canto e pianoforte. A cura di Mario Parenti (Milan, 1963), pl. no. 42602, 4–5.

6. Giuseppe Verdi, *Simon Boccanegra* . . . Opera completa per canto e pianoforte. (Milan), pl. no. 47372, 1–7.

7. On this harmonic shift, see also Budden, *The Operas*, vol. 2, 43.

8. See, for instance, ibid., 450.

9. Published in Alessandro Luzio, ed., *Carteggi verdiani*, vol. 2 (Rome, 1935), 67.

10. Budden, *The Operas*, vol. 2, 450.

11. Martin Chusid, "The Organization of Scenes with Arias: Verdi's Cavatinas and Romanzas," in *Atti del I° congresso internazionale di studi verdiani* (Parma, 1969): 59–66; see 61–62.

12. Philip Gossett, "Verdi, Ghislanzoni, and *Aida*: The Uses of Convention," *Critical Inquiry* 1 (1974): 291–334; see 301–6.

13. Giuseppe Verdi, *Il trovatore*. Opera completa per canto e pianoforte . . . A cura di Mario Parenti (Milan, 1963), pl. no. 42315, 38–42.

14. See chapter 1, 27.

15. See David Lawton, "Verdi, Cavallini, and the Clarinet Solo in *La forza del destino*," in *Verdi. Bollettino dell'Istituto di studi verdiani*, vol. 2, no. 6 (Parma, 1966), 1723–48, esp. 1726–27.

CHAPTER 7

16. Jospeh Kerman, "Verdi's Use of Recurring Themes"; see chapter 1, 25 and 30.

17. Kerman, p. 496.

18. For an acute analysis of this passage, see David Rosen, "'Gonfio di gioia ho il core (piange)': Verdi's Use of Deception," an unpublished paper given at the Irvine conference mentioned in the unnumbered note on p. 127.

19. See Budden, *The Operas*, vol. 2, 453.

20. For a complete modern reprint of the 1862 music, see Federico Mompellio, "Musica provvisoria per *La forza del destino*," in *Verdi*. Bollettino dell'Istituto di studi verdiani, vol. 2, no. 6 (Parma, 1966), 1611–80, esp. 1619–20.

21. See Massimo Bruni, "Funzionalità drammatica dell'accordo di quarta e sesta nello stile di Verdi," in *Atti del I° congresso internazionale di studi verdiani* (Parma, 1969), 36–39.

22. On this duet, and especially on the organization of its third section and the term *parola scenica*, see chapter 6, in particular 114–23.

23. On the affinities (and differences) between the opening melodic phrase of this Cabaletta and a passage in Donizetti's *Poliuto*, see Budden, *The Operas*, vol. 2, 42.

24. A good example of this "breaking from within" of the conventional structure—one that involves various levels—is the Act I Rigoletto-Gilda duet.

25. Once again, the idea of linking directly—at the interval of a semitone or whole tone (as is the case in *La forza del destino*)—the conclusion of a tonally stable set-piece with an ensuing recitative is also taken up in *Aida*, again in the third act, at the end of the Cabaletta in the Aida-Radamès duet ("Ma dimmi. . .").

26. See Péter Pál Várnai, "Leonora és Don Alvaro," in *Verdi*. Bollettino dell'Istituto di studi verdiani, vol. 2, no. 6 (Parma, 1966), 1681–1710.

CHAPTER 8

VERDI'S MUSICAL THOUGHT: AN EXAMPLE FROM *MACBETH*

I SHOULD FIRST clarify the terms of the discussion; what I mean by *musical thought* when writing about a composer such as Verdi, whose production—at least to a casual observer—will suggest no association with either philosophical matters or cultural movements (and still less with manifestos): a body of work that even today is often referred to as "popular," in both the best and the most derogatory senses of that word. What is more, the object of my discussion always liked to portray himself as a man devoid of culture, as the preeminent *musicus practicus*, without intellectual pretensions, strongly resistant to any theoretical definition of his artistic activity.[1]

Long familiarity with Verdi's operas, all of them; the by now inveterate habit of considering them—both in the theater, during live performance, and by studying the scores—as if I encountered them for the first time; an almost daily contact with his letters, whose reproductions we are collecting at the Istituto nazionale di studi verdiani in Parma: all this accumulated experience convinces me ever more strongly that the truth of the man and his work lies not only in a profound commitment toward his art and its cultural function but also in an extremely clear vision of *how* to fulfill his mission as an artist, that is, in the full awareness of the means—both musical and cultural—through which to realize his art.

During the period in which Verdi wrote his first opera, *Oberto, conte di San Bonifacio*—a score that occupied him, with interruptions, for at least three or four years (from January 1836 to November 1839)—the composer affirmed to himself that it would be in musical theater, and *only* in musical theater, that his artistic personality could manifest itself fully; and he received magnificent confirmation of this fact through the international success of *Nabucco* in the years following its Milanese premiere in 1842. Slower and more gradual, however, was his gathering awareness of the means and methods through which to realize his artistic personality. The discovery of a personal, authentic voice took place through a series of experiences that were diverse at both the theatrical and the stylistic level: the operas from *Nabucco* to *Macbeth* (1847). It was fundamentally through these works that Verdi succeeded in acquiring an unmistakeably individual musico-dramatic idiom. Yet, notwithstanding the stylistic variety of this period—a variety dictated in part by external circumstances—the development took place at a steady pace. The experiences acquired through the composition of these early operas became a sort of stylistic storage-point to which Verdi would return in the years to come, making use in a variety of ways of the experiences thus acquired. By the time he faced Shakespearean drama for the first time, he had at his disposal an array of possibilities and, especially, enough experience of the musical theater to grasp immediately what the English dramatist would demand of him. This contact with Shakespeare was also fundamental in revealing to Verdi the necessity of a clearly perceivable continuity in the unfolding of the score and especially of establishing precise connections between the pivotal moments of the drama.

By the time he wrote *Macbeth*, Verdi's musico-dramatic language was determined by a fundamental principle: what mattered above all was the *overall* dimension of the work and, at the same time, its inner coherence. Verdi was concerned with creating a work of art in which each element of the operatic event—dramatic organization, poetic structure of the verbal text, articulation of the score, scenic movement, scenery, costumes, lighting—contributed in exact measure (that is, in the measure precisely corresponding to its function) to the total realization of the drama.[2] It was the task of a musical dramatist to find the right balance between these components, something undertaken as much during the compositional process as in preparations for the performance; or at least it was the task that Verdi set himself and toward whose achievement he always strove.

A thorough understanding of this conception of musical theater will emerge only if we accept its uniqueness within the Italian operatic tradition. In the operas of the great composers who immediately preceded Verdi—Rossini, Bellini, and Donizetti—there may sometimes emerge a sense of musical unity but, if and when it happens, it is always empirical (if not necessarily fortuitous); it is not, in other words, the result of a conscious and careful search, the consequence of a well-defined cultural attitude. In nineteenth-century Italian opera the tradition of considering the closed number—aria, ensemble, concertato, chorus, or finale—as the unit of dramatic rhythm remained fundamentally intact. It goes without saying that this attitude was simply a continuation of that of eighteenth-century *opera seria*. This conception is clearly reflected in the composing process of most operas: they were created number by number, not necessarily—in fact hardly ever—following the order of the plot, and with the performers who would create the leading roles close at hand; the basic structures of the score—the vocal lines—were modeled on these performers.[3]

Verdi, who would never entirely abandon some features of this conception (for example, the trying-out with singers of their vocal parts[4]), sought determinedly and tenaciously to overcome the basic fragmentation of discourse resulting from it; to use his own words, he strove to avoid writing "[. . .] mosaic music, devoid of style and character."[5] Musico-dramatic unity was the goal toward which the composer strove throughout his long career, and he did so with an absolutely coherent clarity of vision; to the extent that one could define this concept as distinctive and characterizing of the entire corpus of Verdi's art.

Like any true dramatist, Verdi well knew that the essence of theater consists not merely in defining the various characters' individuality but rather in their interaction, in the confrontation of their aspirations and their passions: he had, from the beginning of his career, an evolutionary, dynamic conception of the theatrical event. This explains why he adopted and then immediately abandoned the idea of identifying the principal characters of the drama by means of "recurring themes," a technique with which he experimented for the first time, in a systematic way, in *I due Foscari* of 1844.[6] In this opera, each of the principals is characterized by an instrumental motto that—identical each time—signals their entrance onstage; these mottos are supposed to identify the characters' fundamental psychological features and their function in the drama: Jacopo's resigned sadness, Lucrezia's passionate vehemence, the old doge's noble dignity, and, most important, the evil plotting of the Council of Ten. Verdi, who was to use the technique of "recurring themes" throughout his career, immediately understood that the system—at least in the way he used it in *I due Foscari*—would not function dramatically: once presented, these mottos—true instrumental "visiting cards"—are in no way susceptible to development, to articulation; their systematic use leads to stasis in the dramatic tension, to a rigidity in the dynamic of the action.

It was only with *Macbeth* that Verdi began to apply in a systematic way the basic technique of his musico-dramatic language. I do not intend here to investigate the extent to which Shakespearian theater influenced the emergence of this conception. But it is certain that the two phenomena are related and that the one played a determining role in the affirmation of the other.

To establish connections among the key dramatic moments of the plot, Verdi used the most basic elements of musical language: simple pitch levels; brief, incisive rhythmic figures; isolated instrumental timbres. He understood that the simpler the units of musical language, the richer their possible articulation in dramatic terms, so long as these units are recognizable through their temporal configuration, that is, through their duration.

A system of this type obviously will not determine all the *situtazioni*[7] of the plot and has the additional advantage of not predetermining all the events. As we shall see from *Macbeth*, it involves only the moments that are dramatically relevant, the hinges of the dramatic tension.

MACBETH'S covert, almost unconfessed aspirations to power, his desire for the Scottish throne, are continually echoed, nurtured, and stimulated by the cynical urgings of his wife, the only leading character in the entire Verdian corpus who has no first name, who is merely "Lady Macbeth"; the couple's aspirations and destinies are inseparably linked. The gradual revelation of this thirst for power culminates in the moment when Macbeth—after having murdered the sleeping Duncan—returns to the stage, hands bloody, and announces to his wife that "the deed is done." In the libretto, this climactic moment is marked with the protagonist's words "Tutto è finito!" In the score the phrase is declaimed as shown in example 8.1.

EXAMPLE 8.1

The essential musical elements here are the rhythmic pattern and, especially, the pitches: C and D♭.[8] Verdi stressed these pitches to the maximum by repeating them in the orchestra and, through a development of the melodic line, by leading the music into F minor, the key in which the duet between the two principals begins (example 8.2). This duet, from a dramatic point of view, has the primary purpose of making manifest and developing in the minds of both characters the consequences of their criminal act: Macbeth already tormented by remorse, Lady Macbeth derisive and cynical about his fears.

EXAMPLE 8.2

It was therefore necessary to give the entire duet a unity achieved by musical means and to make it thus dramatically relevant, to indicate its connection with the key moment in the preceding scene, Macbeth's exclamation "Tutto è finito!" Verdi needed, moreover, to define the dramatic elements that would eventually lead to the denouement: from the murder of Duncan spring all the other crimes, Lady Macbeth's delirium, and finally the death of the protagonist.

The duet is structured in an entirely conventional manner, following principles already canonized in the operas of Rossini:[9] each of the four sections is distinguished from the others by meter, tempo, and keys. The *tempo d'attacco* is in F minor, Allegro in 6/8 ("Fatal mia donna, un murmure"); the central movement in B♭ major, Andantino in 3/8 ("Allor questa voce"); a second Allegro, as *tempo di mezzo*, in 6/8, this time in D minor ("Il pugnal là riportate . . ."); and finally the Stretta ("Vieni altrove! ogni sospetto"), again in F minor, Allegro in ¢. These four sections are already characterized in the libretto by means of different meters:[10] *settenari* (alternately *sdruccioli* and *piani*) for the first section; *senari doppi* for the second; *ottonari* for the third; and *ottonari* again for the last. What is new, however, is the *manner* in which the musical language is articulated, not only within each section, but also in relation to the key phrase of the preceding recitative: Macbeth's "Tutto è finito!" by which—as we have seen—the duet is introduced. We have already seen how Verdi links it, in purely musical terms, to the first section of the duet. In fact, the second section, "Allor questa voce," opens with a phrase for the protagonist that repeats the intervals and declamation of "Tutto è finito!" a fifth lower (example 8.3). The orchestral beginning to the

EXAMPLE 8.3

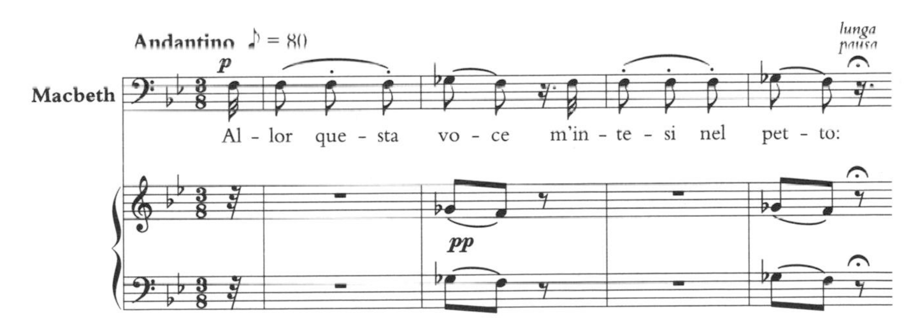

third section of the duet also echoes Macbeth's phrase, this time inverting its melodic direction, D–C♯–D (example 8.4a). Within these sections the relationship of affinity and contrast between the two principals is occasionally brought to the fore, using traditional conventions to characterize their negative and positive aspects. Thus, in the first section, the groups of four sixteenth-notes,

EXAMPLE 8.4a

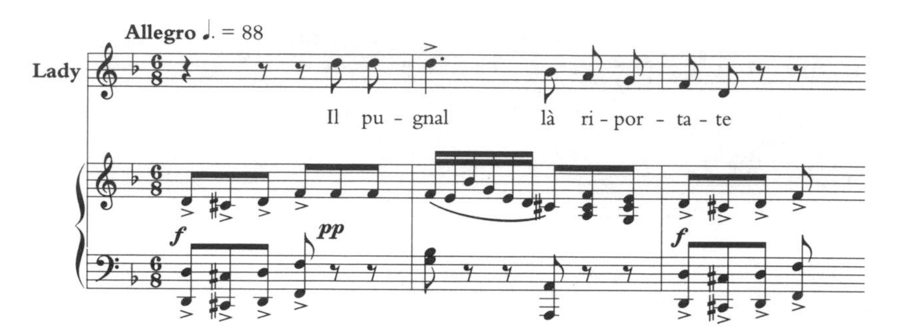

preceded by the acciaccatura at the word "Follie!" and, in the second section, the use of unison between voice and orchestra ("Ma dimmi altra voce" etc.) serve to characterize Lady Macbeth's abrasive irony; they sharply contrast with the broad melodic phrase (example 8.4b) that indentifies the protagonist's remorse ("Com'angeli d'ira").

EXAMPLE 8.4b

EXAMPLE 8.4b, *cont.*

All this is a novelty, in the definition both of characters and of their relationships within the structure of a duet (i.e., within a single "closed number"). But Verdi's aim was to create a musico-dramatic logic that was coherent on a larger scale; he therefore used similar procedures in constructing the closing number, the Finale of this act, thus establishing direct links between its pivotal moments and other dramatically significant moments that had preceded it.

The Finale is built as follows:

1. a "neutral" recitative between Macduff and Banco. Macduff goes off to wake Duncan;
2. Banco's arioso, which expresses his premonitions of coming misfortune; this section moves through C minor, F minor, (C minor), D♭ major, A♭ major, and C major;
3. Macduff reenters precipitously: he has discovered the horrible deed; words desert him; Banco goes to see for himself. Macduff calls everyone onstage; Banco announces the murder of Duncan. In this section the premonitions Banco expressed in the preceding section come true:

the reality of death is before them. And the succession of keys is exactly the same as in that section, though now they are scanned rhythmically with the "figure of death": ♩ 𝄾· ♬ ♩ 𝄾· ♬ | ♩ [11]

4. everyone explodes in indignation; this feeling is caused by Macbeth's crime, and therefore the fateful exclamation "Tutto è finito!" (C–D♭–C) is repeated—at the corresponding tonal level—to the words "Schiudi o terra!" (F–G♭–F);
5. there follows a "Preghiera," sung a cappella by the soloists, who are gradually joined by the chorus; a crescendo leads to a "Grandioso" passage for soloists, chorus, and orchestra, in which the tension created by the preceding episodes unfolds into a broad melodic phrase whose rhythm offers a further development of the figure at the start of the episode; through a polyphonic elaboration of the basic idea we reach the final Stretta, in whose closing exclamation ("Gran Dio!"), sung by the soloists, we can hear the final transformation of this rhythmic idea.

The dramatic conclusion of the tragedy is not so much the death of the protagonist but rather the "Gran scena del sonnambulismo" (the musical number corresponding to the "Sleepwalking scene" in Shakespeare's play)—the moment in which Lady Macbeth, who has mocked her husband's sense of guilt, relives the murder of Duncan and the crimes that followed it, in a disturbed, nightmare-ridden sleep, interspersed with a death-rattle that is also a sigh. Verdi was fully aware of the dramatic importance of this scene and of its direct connection to the first-act duet; he even wrote about it to the librettist Cammarano, in connection with a performance in Naples in 1848: "Note that there are two principal numbers in the opera: the duet between the *Lady and her husband* and the sleepwalking scene. If these numbers fail, then the opera is ruined. And these pieces must absolutely not be sung: they must be acted out and declaimed with a very hollow and veiled voice; otherwise, they won't be able to make any effect."[12] The Sleepwalking scene is preceded, as in Shakespeare's play, by a long dialogue between the doctor and Lady Macbeth's lady-in-waiting. This dialogue prepares the entrance of the soloist by retelling previous events; its last phrase is sung by the lady-in-waiting who, in answer to the doctor's question of why Lady Macbeth rubs her hands, replies: "Lavarsi crede" (she thinks she is washing them). These words are declaimed on exactly the same pitch (C and D♭) and with the same dotted rhythm as Macbeth's phrase that introduced the duet, "Tutto è finito!" The dialogue between the lady-in-waiting and the doctor unfolds in F minor, and the recitative ends with a unison C in the orchestra, a pitch that seems to be a dominant about to resolve to its tonic, F. We immediately move, however, to D♭ major, which is the key of the following scene. Here Verdi tranfers to the structural level (that of a key scheme within a section) the pitch succession that had characterized moments that were dramatically significant at the beginning of the action (Macbeth's exclamation "Tutto è finito!"), and through this identity he established a profound dramatic connection between them. But there is more.

In the opening section of the first-act duet, the voices of the two soloists were accompanied in unison in the orchestra by the penetrating and unmistakeable timbre of the English horn. In other words, the timbre characterized the situation through its distinctive color. The timbre of this instrument returns in the Sleepwalking scene, to punctuate with a descending semitone, a true musical lament, the soloist's brief, anguished phrases (example 8.5). And this is a final way of making evident the profound connection between the two episodes.

Example 8.5

EXAMPLE 8.5, *cont.*

AMONG ALL the operas that might have served to illustrate my central point, I have chosen *Macbeth* for two reasons: first, because the Shakespearean model offered Verdi an exemplary dramatic structure on which to build the logic of his own musical theater; and second, because *Macbeth* is the first score, chronologically speaking, in which the composer systematically employed the organizing principles of his musical thought. I should perhaps repeat that these principles in no sense aspire to control *all* the dramatic relationships, still less *all* the moments of the score (as will happen with Wagnerian *Leitmotiven*); instead, their purpose is to characterize, distinguish between, and define merely those that are dramatically significant; above all they serve to establish a clear, easily identifiable connection between these moments, thus determining their mutual dependence.

In this way Verdi forged the musico-dramatic unity of his scores. This unity is, in my opinion, his most original artistic achievement; and it is thanks to the profound logic that determines the organization of these scores that they have such an impact—today as much as ever—on the culture and the sensibility of our time.

Notes

1. A well-argued and well-documented attack on this often repeated opinion can be found in Mary-Jane Matz, "Verdi: The Roots of the Tree," in *Verdi*. Bollettino dell'Istituto di studi verdiani, vol. 3, no. 7 (Parma, 1969), 333–64.

2. It is all the more striking that the obviously similar conception, that of Wagner's as theorized, for example, in *Oper und Drama*, came about at more-or-less the same time and thus in a completely independent manner. The basic difference between the two composers lies not so much in the conception behind their works as in the works themselves, in the difference of musical means they used to realize their conceptions—above all, in the different sense of time.

3. On Bellini's use of this composing technique while working on the score of *I puritani*, see chapter 10.

4. See, for instance, his rehearsal of Desdemona's "Willow Song" with the first interpreter of the role, Romilda Pantaleoni, as witnessed in his letter to Giulio Ricordi of 18 October 1886, published in Pierluigi Petrobelli and Franca Cella, eds., *Giuseppe Verdi–Giulio Ricordi: corrispondenza e immagini 1881/1890* (Milan, 1981), 51.

5. The sentence is quoted by Carlo Gatti (though with no specific reference) in his introduction to the facsimile of the *Rigoletto* sketches, *L'abbozzo del Rigoletto di Giuseppe Verdi*, edizione fuori commercio a cura del Ministero della Cultura Popolare (Milan, 1941). See also chapter 2, n. 2.

6. For a discussion of "recurring themes," see Joseph Kerman, "Verdi's Use of Recurring Themes" (see the postscript to chapter 1, on p. 30).

7. In the language of nineteenth-century Italian opera, *situazione* defines the moment of the plot that corresponds to a musical "number."

8. As I state in the introduction many ideas that recur in this book are the results of discussions based on seminar reports, with various students in various countries at differ-

ent times. I should like to mention in connection with this chapter Professor Elliott Antokoletz, who was a member of my Verdi seminar at the Graduate Center of the City University of New York in the fall term of 1970. His work in that seminar has since appeared in his article "Verdi's Dramatic Use of Harmony and Tonality in *Macbeth*," *In Theory Only* 4, no. 6 (1978): 17–28.

9. For a definition of the basic structure of a nineteenth-century Italian opera duet, see Philip Gossett, "Verdi, Ghislanzoni, and the Use of Convention," mentioned in chapter 6, n. 2.

10. For the exact meaning of these terms, see the note on Italian prosody at the beginning of this book.

11. For a definition and a discussion of the use of this rhythmic figure, see Frits Noske, "Verdi and the Musical Figure of Death," *Atti del III° congresso internazionale di studi verdiani* (Parma, 1974), 349–86; reprinted in Noske, *The Signifier and the Signified—Studies in the Operas of Mozart and Verdi* (The Hague, 1977; reprint, Oxford, 1990), 171–214.

12. For both the Italian and the English texts, see David Rosen and Andrew Porter, eds., *Verdi's "Macbeth." A Sourcebook* (New York, 1984), 67.

CHAPTER 9

THE MUSICO-DRAMATIC CONCEPTION OF GLUCK'S *ALCESTE* (1767)

ALCESTE holds a rather unusual place in the history of music. The preface to the opera, signed by Gluck and written under the strong influence of Calzabigi, is cited time and again;[1] but interest in the prose that precedes the printed score is not matched by an equally lively concern for what follows—the opera itself. Why is this?

The preface to *Alceste* offers all the advantages that writings similar in character and function carry with them: the clear, firm adoption of a stance, in turn clearly set against what had until then been taken and practiced as normal in the cultural milieu to which the document belongs—in this case, that of musical theater. There is, in this text, condemnation of the indiscriminate use of certain formal principles in general use at the time and a powerful proposal for different, more coherent criteria: ones invoked with reference to rational or even philosophical principles that represented at the time the avant-garde position in contemporary thought: I refer, of course, to the principles of the Enlightenment.[2] A rejection of vocal virtuosity; a repudiation of the incoherence arising from the predominance and indiscriminate use of the da capo aria; and above all a rebellion against the lack of a conscious, sought-after coherence between the various parts of the scenic action (stylistic peculiarities all prevalent in the field of Italian *opera seria*): these are the principles invoked by making appeal to clarity and reason, those principles that informed the many cultural activities of the Encyclopedists. Only by applying these principles to musical theater did Gluck think that a composer could attain the goal and ultimate object of his activity: to reach "a beautiful simplicity."[3]

It is worth recalling that so far as musical theater is concerned, principles of clarity and logical coherence were hardly invoked for the first time in the preface to *Alceste*. But it is significant that these principles were called for not by musicians and writers on music but by literary scholars and other people of culture. To offer a single example, the same principles inform Algarotti's *Saggio sopra l'opera in musica*, published fifteen years earlier. There is no doubt that Gluck had in mind the criteria and the aspirations of the Enlightenment in formulating his "manifesto"—as, perhaps even more, did Calzabigi, who during his stay in Paris had the chance to encounter and assimilate the new ideas. The preface to *Alceste* thus aimed at satisfying broadly intellectual rather than merely musical and artistic needs; and these needs were expressed not by the opera audience at large (still less by devotees of *opera seria*) but rather by a small circle of cultural elite, who were eager to see this composite and many-faceted theatrical phenomenon conform to the canons of classical theater—in particular to the Aristotelian principle of unity.

How, then, did Gluck put these principles into practice? In what ways is the score of *Alceste* different from an *opera seria* of the time? In my opinion, simple rejection of the formal principles and stylistic peculiarities that the preface lists—da capo arias and vocal virtuosity—cannot adequately characterize this score. Even if there is no self-indulgent display of vocal ornament, virtuosity of vocal intonation and agility are frequent. So far as rejection of the da capo aria is concerned, it is worth recalling that the protagonist's aria in the first act, "Ombre, larve," ends with a literal repeat of the opening eighteen measures;[4] indeed, symmetries and parallel returns of sections and phrases are the dominating structural principle of the score. Where, then, lies the novelty of this musical theater? To answer this question, we need to analyze closely some passages from the opera; and we might take the first scenes as an example.

The "Intrada,"[5] the instrumental prelude that establishes the *Stimmung* of the theatrical action, ends on the dominant of the key in which the true action begins: an A-major chord leads directly to the D-major trumpet calls (mm. 1–7)[6] that announce the entrance of the herald. The latter proclaims in recitative that King Admetus has reached the end of his life, that there is no hope of his recovery (mm. 8–28).

The subsequent choral exclamation, "Ah, di questo afflitto regno,"[7] marks the beginning of a long episode that takes up the entire first scene of the opera and in which this choral phrase has a predominant, even characterizing role. It is at this point that one notices the first divergences between the printed libretto and the score. In Calzabigi's libretto the initial choral quatrain (in *ottonari*) is followed by a second quatrain in *quinari doppi*, given to "Una voce"; a brief monologue for Evander, in which Admetus's confidant invites the dismayed people to consult the oracle at the temple of Apollo, is framed by the repetition of the chorus's two opening lines ("Ah di questo afflitto regno / Giusti Dei, che mai sarà"); a further quatrain, again of *quinari doppi* and given to "Una voce," is followed by a final statement of the chorus's first line, which is in turn interrupted by Evander's announcement that Alceste, the queen, is about to emerge from the palace.[8]

Gluck did not merely follow these cyclic points offered by Calzabigi's text, he developed them; but he did so with one important difference. Alceste's confidante Ismene (who is mentioned in the libretto as onstage but not singing) and Evander assume in the score the function of "coryphaei": Gluck gives them, respectively, the first and second quatrains of *quinari doppi* destined for "Una voce." What is more, these characters intervene with entire phrases, with repetitions and solo (or, rather, two-voice unison) interpolations in the choral sections, in such a way that the larger musical structure of the scene is different from that imagined by the librettist.

The organization of the first choral phrase, and its alternation with those of the two soloists, is particularly interesting.[9] The entire passage takes up seventeen and a half measures, if we include the instrumental conclusion. The three opening choral measures are followed by the soloists (one and a half measures), the chorus (one measure), the soloists again (also one measure, and an intensification of their first statement), and then again the chorus (one and a half measures, also an intensified reprise of its first statement). The remaining six measures, for chorus alone, bring the episode to its point of greatest tension (third quarter of m. 39) and then die down, concluding with four instrumental measures (example 9.1).

EXAMPLE 9.1

Example 9.1, *cont.*

Example 9.1, *cont.*

In light of the basically homophonic part writing, the vertical disposition of the voices—the harmony—assumes great importance, as does the relationship between one statement and another. This relationship is essentially rhetorical, in that each repetition increases the intensity and thus augments the tension. In a style that—to repeat—is essentially homophonic and in which the voice leading is essentially stepwise, each variant, each dissonance and harmonic modification, assumes great importance.

The short "dialogue" between the soloists and chorus, inserted after the opening three choral measures, thus forms a section in itself and serves the purpose of emphasizing that the two "coryphaei" voices are an integral part of the episode, since the same rhetorical principle is applied both to them and to the chorus. Proof of this comes later in the scene, in the reprise of the initial chorus (mm. 57–97),[10] where the "dialogue" between the chorus and soloists is deleted without creating any feeling of omission or break (example 9.2).

EXAMPLE 9.2

Soprano
Alto
Tenore
Basso
Coro
Ah di que-sto af-flit-to re-gno, di que-sto af-flit-to re-gno,
Ah di que-sto af-flit-to re-gno, di que-sto af-flit-to re-gno,
f
giu-sti Dei, che mai, che mai sa-rà!
giu-sti Dei, che mai, che mai sa-rà!
Più
Andante

The episodes entrusted to the two "coryphaei"—first in rhythmic unison ("Ah per noi del ciel lo sdegno," mm. 47–57), then for Ismene alone (mm. 69–93)[11] and, in the second part of the scene, for Evander (mm. 162–80)[12]—are thus no more than textural and timbral variants of the choral episodes: they are constructed basically from the same material; and their harmonic and rhythmic language, their phrase articulation, their progression and relationships are those established by Gluck at the opening of the scene, in the first choral passage. In this way the composer achieved—through musical means used with great economy and subtlety, and above all by making use of the rhetorical principle of analogy—a continuity of discourse that stretches over a substantial section of time.

The importance of this conception of musico-dramatic time can be seen from the following diagram, in which I indicate as "C" the choral episode that includes the soloists, and as "c" those abbrieviated episodes given only to the chorus:

C	Duo	c	Solo Ismene	c	"Aria di Pantomimo"
mm. 29–47	mm. 47–57	mm. 57–69	mm. 69–93	mm. 93–105	mm. 106–27

Recitative Evander	C	Solo Evander	c (beginning)	Recitative Evander
mm. 128–44	mm. 145–62	mm. 162–80	mm. 180–82	mm. 182–97

If we bear in mind that section C is then repeated one final time in the concluding section of the next scene,[13] after Alceste's recitative and aria, "Io non chiedo, eterni Dei" (framed by two choral episodes given to two groups placed at the extreme sides of the stage), and if we consider that this final reprise is in turn concluded by a choral Allegro[14] whose material is clearly an elaboration of the homophonic duo between the two "coryphaei" (mm. 47–57 of the preceding scene), we gain an idea of the extent of the temporal arch within which Gluck constructed dramatic tension.

From this analysis of the opening scenes of *Alceste* we can see that there are two principles at work, on two structural levels. The first concerns the organization of single episodes, of moments that are musically enclosed. By deliberately making a limited, sparing use of the basic elements of musical language, Gluck proceeds by literally repeating phrases and sections; or, more frequently, by developing them through slight alterations; or by preserving one element of the language (usually the rhythmic articulation) between one section and the next, and varying another (usually the harmony); or by taking the melodic idea or rhythmic formula of a section and making it the characterizing element of a subsequent section, whether or not it is adjacent; or by repeating a phrase in stepwise motion in order to create both tension and continuity simultaneously. The result of all these procedures is an expansion of the temporal dimension of the musical discourse, thus creating important connections both within sections and between one section and another.

The second structural principle concerns a higher level and involves both of the two scenes examined. By following the libretto in consciously employing literal (or slightly abbreviated) repetitions of entire sections, the sense of continuity and coherence within single musical moments is extended across scenes. In other words, Gluck brings the same principle that he had used within single musical moments to a higher structural level. If we examine other parts of *Alceste* from this perspective, we can see substantially the same process; this is especially true of the choral episodes and also of some that are purely musical, such as the "Arie di Pantomimo." This organizing principle is not applied to individual arias, since these "closed numbers" are in turn embedded in larger organisms, within which they assert themselves by way of contrast, through difference of language and organization. In the end, even this last is a means of creating tension and variety while at the same time linking adjacent moments in the action. In any case, the result tends always in the same direction: to create a temporal dimension that is larger than the single musical episode, the single section.

In my opinion, it is here that we must search for the extraordinary novelty of *Alceste*, of the new musical theater that Gluck instituted with this opera. Here lies its importance in the history not only of theatrical music but of music in general. There is no doubt that a desire to re-create in music the theater of ancient Greece was the starting point of the entire operation. It is hardly fortuitous that the frontispiece of the 1769 printed score published in Vienna reads "ALCESTE. Tragedia messa in musica dal Signore Cavagliere Cristoforo Gluck," thus echoing the 1767 printed libretto, "ALCESTE. Tragedia per musica," and prefiguring the unusual coupling of terms on the frontispiece of the printed score in its 1776 Paris edition, "ALCESTE. Tragedie. Opera en trois actes par M. le Chevalier Gluck."[15]

As always happens with decisive events in history, the consequences were not immediate, but they led to a conception of musical time that we can without doubt call our own.

Notes

1. The preface is found on p. [3] of the score: *Alceste.* Tragedia Messa in musica dal Signore Cavagliere Cristoforo Gluck. Dedicata a Sua Altezza Reale, l'Arciduca Pietro Leopoldo Gran-Duca di Toscana, etc. In Vienna, nella stamperia aulica di Giovanni Tommaso de Trattner MDCCLXIX.

2. Ibid., p. [4].

3. For a discussion of *Alceste* in the context of contemporary cultural movements, see my "L'*Alceste* di Calzabigi e Gluck: L'illuminismo e l'opera," in *Memorie e contributi alla musica dal Medioevo all'età moderna offerti a Federico Ghisi, Quadrivium* 12 (1971): 279–93.

4. For the musical examples in this chapter I have used the vocal score: Chr. W. Gluck, *Alceste* (Wiener Fassung von 1767). Tragedia in drei Akten von Raniero de'

Calzabigi. Klavierauszug von Herbert Viecenz. Kassel-Basel-London, Bärenreiter, BA 2292.

5. Ibid., 1–6. The title "Intrada" is found in the printed score (see n. 1).

6. *Alceste* (see n. 4), 7.

7. Ibid., 8–9.

8. *Alceste*. Tragedia per musica. In Vienna. Nella stamperia di Ghelen, 1767, 2–3. The copy I consulted is in I-Rsc (Biblioteca musicale di S. Cecilia in Rome).

9. *Alceste* (see n. 4), 8–9.

10. Ibid., 11.

11. Ibid., 12.

12. Ibid., 18.

13. Ibid., 40.

14. Ibid., 41–45.

15. Published "A Paris, Chez Des Lauriers M^{d} de Papier rue St. Honoré à coté de celle des Provaires." The copy I consulted is in I-Bc (Civico Museo Bibliografico Musicale in Bologna), FF 160.

CHAPTER 10

NOTES ON BELLINI'S POETICS: APROPOS OF *I PURITANI*

CRITICAL EVALUATION of that aspect of Italian culture usually called *melodramma*—the operas written by nineteenth-century Italian composers—represents a vast, unexplored territory for musicology. This statement might perhaps seem paradoxical given the extent of the repertory and its amazing, ever-increasing vitality (we need think only of the recurring "renaissances," "revivals," and "rehabilitations" that make up the programs of the world's great opera houses), but it will be very clear to anyone who cares to glance at the bibliography devoted to this area or to the work of its most significant figures—a bibliography markedly lacking in serious scholarship. And perhaps the reason for this paucity is to be found precisely in the "popularity" of the repertory, in the immediate effect it continues to have (though in less casual terms than one might imagine) on the public at large: it operates principally on the listeners' emotions, addressing itself directly to their sensibilities in the least sophisticated manner. This state of affairs, however, should not prevent us from confronting and evaluating *melodramma* with precise cultural and critical tools. Only a detailed analysis of these cultural events and a rigorous historical "placing" of each of them within the work of their creator will allow us to find the "message" (a much-abused term, perhaps, but still useful) that the composer intended to send us, and so to evaluate its importance.

As I have mentioned elsewhere,[1] this method of approaching *melodramma* can cause considerable surprises, reveal unexpected connections, and allow us to grasp more fully, to understand and appreciate in a truer and more penetrating manner, the genuine dramatic, musical, and human values hidden within the genre.

The works of Vincenzo Bellini are among those that await such analytical and critical study: very few publications devoted to the composer go beyond apologetic exultations of the work;[2] very few even try to avoid becoming entangled in the murky sentimental adventures of the ardent young composer; most end up as laudatory, indiscriminate paeans based on an instinctive feeling of affinity rather than on concrete understanding of the musical and cultural values in their historical context.[3]

A first, basic step toward deeper appreciation of Bellini's work might lie in an attempt to reconstruct the composer's ideas on how to write music, especially music in the theater; to study his way of conceiving the relationships between words and music—in short, to examine what we define as the artist's "poetics." However, before engaging in study of the scores, we need to reconstruct those ideas through reading what the composer said or wrote; for although Bellini was by nature averse to systematizing his conceptual ideas, he nevertheless possessed a clear, precise vision of how to proceed in artistic matters.

Bellini's ideas on opera and on the relationship between words and music became precisely defined, clearly formulated, and repeatedly stated while sketching out the score—while working, in collaboration with the librettist, on the structural organization of the literary text, and particularly while finding its precise verbal formulation. And so we can gain definite, dependable information from reading his correspondence with librettists. It is from the instructions, suggestions, and requests that Bellini gave, explicitly and sometimes even peremptorily, to his collaborators (a tone that surprises in a personality such as his, by nature gentle, sometimes even ingratiating) that we can derive circumstantial information, thus distancing ourselves from the insidious vagueness of the "legends."[4]

It should come as no surprise that the quotations forming the nucleus of this chapter date almost exclusively from the period during which *I puritani* was composed and thus from the final stages of Bellini's career. The composer's creative span was too short to show any marked alteration in attitude or even achievement: the principles that guide the composition of *Il pirata* remain the same for *I puritani*, even if by the time of the latter they had assumed a more mature, distinct form, and the composer had a greater and more exact understanding of them. In *I puritani*, however, one can find hints of a new sensibility, of attitudes that suggest directions the composer's genius might have taken had he lived longer.

It is worth remembering that Bellini's circumstances during the period of *I puritani* were in a certain sense favorable to our inquiry. Arriving in Paris in the summer of 1833, after a year in London during which his success as a composer was equaled only by his social success, Bellini, at the height of his fame, undertook to write a new *melodramma* for the Théâtre Italien. His relationship with Felice Romani, the librettist of *Norma* and *La sonnambula*, was then rather strained, so he was obliged to search out a "local" man of letters to help him prepare the new opera. In the salon of Cristina Trivulzio, Princess Belgioioso, the alluring Lombard "exile" who gathered around her many of the most representative cultural figures of the period, Bellini met Carlo Pepoli, a Bolognese count and man of letters to whom Giacomo Leopardi had dedicated one of his *Canti* and who was exiled in Paris after having taken part in the Romagna uprisings of 1831.[5] Here was the "poet" who would sketch out the text Bellini needed. We do not know the exact date of the meeting, but from the composer's correspondence we learn that the choice of subject for the new libretto followed rather than preceded the event. On 11 March 1834 Bellini wrote to Florimo: "In the meantime I want to see how Count Pepoli will do this libretto [*libro*] for Paris; I have hopes that he will succeed, perhaps very well, because he writes good verse and has facility in doing so."[6] Clearly, the composer had already tested his librettist's ability;[7] but, as we learn from a postscript to the same letter, the plot had not yet been chosen: "Pepoli has proposed some subjects that seem interesting. One perhaps for Paris, since it is a French play, and the other for Naples. In another letter I will tell you if we decide on one of these."[8]

The matter is taken up again on the following day, in a letter to his friend Barbò in Naples: "I am searching for subjects and hope to find one soon, or rather to choose between the three or four offered me. Count Pepoli will write the poetry for me. He is well known in Italy, and thus there is reason to expect something from him."[9]

The choice of an author of the "poetry" was therefore more important to Bellini than choice of the subject for the opera. Or, better: the choice of "poet" had priority (which does not necessarily mean precedence) over the choice of subject.[10] In all likelihood this priority was common to all Italian opera composers of the early nineteenth century. But, even without the proof that the above quotations offer about the order of events (and such proofs are particularly valuable when dealing with nineteenth-century Italian opera), the practice reveals to us where a composer (whether Bellini or his contemporaries) started when creating an opera.

The *melodramma* of Bellini's time was conceived primarily, almost exclusively, in terms of the vocal parts. More specifically, the opera was "tailored" for the singers who would create the first performance: once a scene—or even simply a single piece—was imagined, the composer needed to try out his music with the voice for whom it had been written, just as one would "try on" a new suit of clothes. When, for example, Bellini described a series of scenes or an act, he almost always referred to the interpreters, to the singer or singers who were to perform the episode, rather than to the name of the characters. His description of the first performance of *Il pirata* is a good case in point:

> Rubini's Sortita [i.e., his first aria] created a furor beyond description, and I got up at least ten times to thank the audience. The prima donna's Cavatina was also applauded; after a chorus of pirates with echo, which pleased through the novelty of my having created the echo so well [. . .] there followed the *scena* and duet for Rubini and Lalande, after which the public all shouted like madmen, making such a noise that we seemed in an inferno; after that came Tamburini's Cavatina, which although applauded pleased little—and then came the finale; the Largo was admired greatly as a fine work of art and, making its effect through the main melody that dominates, was much applauded [. . .][11]

At the end of Bellini's career, a description he gave Florimo of the overall structure of *I puritani* is very similar:

ACT I

1st "Introduzione" made up of military chorus, a prayer sung by the Puritans and Peasant women, etc., etc.
2nd Cavatina for Tamburrini [*sic*]
3rd Duet for Lablache and Grisi
4th Chorus and Cavatina in one movement for Rubini
5th Finale—made up of a brilliant "quartettino" // a trio in two movements *not long* and the Largo second movement has a grand effect, if I'm not mistaken (we could call this a duet since it is between Tamburrini and Rubini and the 2da donna, and she only has some words here and there) and then there is a Largo concertato in which I have just the two basses and Grisi with the chorus, and the Stretta of the finale—.

ACT II

1st Chorus and Romanza for Lablache
2nd Duet for the two basses
3rd Trio for the two basses and Grisi: this is like the quartet from *Nina*, in which the female role has everything; it will, then, seem more-or-less a scene for her
4th Chorus of "dawn or liberty," etc.
5th Scene for Rubini
6th Finale—made up of a duet for Grisi and Rubini, of an ensemble piece, and finally a Cabaletta for the prima donna.[12]

In the same letter, immediately following the above, Bellini speaks of his method of composition: "In the 1st act everything is composed and orchestrated except the trio and "quartettino" of the finale and the duet for Lablache and Grisi, and I haven't orchestrated [these pieces] because Lablache arrived the day before yesterday, and neither Grisi nor Rubini is yet in Paris and I need to try the pieces out with them first."[13]

AGAIN writing to Florimo about the project to bring *I puritani* to Naples (instead of writing a new opera), Bellini proposed Malibran for the part of Elvira: "[. . .] I will have to leave *Paris as soon as I Puritani has gone on stage*, [. . .] *come to Naples and adapt for Malibran and for the rest of the company that opera, perhaps composing some new pieces* when it is deemed necessary by me and Malibran, who will be consulted fully by me, and thus I will make an almost new opera through these transformations; all this will be done at the time when rehearsals begin, and as quickly as possible [. . .]."[14] The structure of the musico-dramatic texture was an immediate consequence of this conception of musical theater: a constant alternation of vocal timbres and thus of "affective" moments that are differentiated but not set against each other and, above all, not necessarily connected by a closely argued dramatic dialectic. Each act is subdivided into various sections, various distinct "scenes," in each of which the singer's voice and the "situation" it delineates (or, better, through which it is delineated) must have complete preeminence and be formally self-contained. Since the basic emotions of these "situations" must be realized with maximum clarity through vocal means (the instruments therefore function as accompaniment, as a necessary but discreet secondary discourse), the words, the verses, have to sculpt the scenic moment, the basic emotional substance of the episode. This is what Bellini asked of Pepoli, but the "poet" could satisfy him only in part: "Pepoli works, and it costs me a good deal of effort to carry him forward; he lacks experience, which is very important."[15] And further on: "Pepoli serves me with true friendship and there is nothing bad in anything he has done for me: he's better than anybody else, but he's not Romani, and a Romani one does not find easily."[16] Romani's uniqueness lay principally in his ability to define exactly through verse the "affective" (the term here has its eighteenth-century meaning, that of an abstract, exemplary emotional model) situation:

> It is true that Romani's illness lessens day by day; but even if he carries on in this way, he won't be able to start work for ten or more days. And if the worst happens, he won't be able to write the libretto for me, and then I'll be desperate; because even though Rossi would write me a good libretto, he could never be a versifier like Romani, especially for me, who is so attached to good words: look in *Pirata* how the verses rather than the situations inspired me, in particular: *Come un angelo celeste*, and thus for me Romani is necessary.[17]

The exact wording of the "affect" is, then, even more important than the content of the dramatic moment in which it is realized.

What is more, Romani always bore in mind the function of his verses; he knew what was entailed in writing poetry for music and for singers, and he also knew how to adapt the plot to these demands:

> It seems that both Romani and I, and also Pollini, lean toward *La straniera* by Arlincourt, and you yourself supplied me with the idea in one of your earlier letters. Romani will not follow the play at all but will gather together all the best situations from the novel, that is to say [. . .]: the arrival of Artur on the island of Montolino—the meeting of Artur with the Straniera at the fountain—Valdebourgo's recognition that the Straniera is his sister and the duel with Artur—the judgment—the wedding—and the death of Artur and the Straniera. All this will be divided into perhaps four very small acts, to give verisimilitude of time and place. Romani is working very hard at it but says that without a good tenor for the part of Artur there

> will be serious problems, because we will then have to give the part of Artur to Tamburini, the Straniera to Lalande, Isoletta to Unger; the part of Valdeburgo (which is very interesting) will go to Reina, but if Rubini comes, would be given to Tamburrini, and Montolino [will go] to a second bass, and the abbott of S. Irene to Biondini.—If Rubini comes, the plot would seem to be almost certain of success, since it is full of situations, all new and grandiose; but without Rubini I am cast down [. . .].[18]

Bellini thus conceived of opera as a chain of "situations," of abstract moments, linked by a tenuous plot, and—above all—devoid of internal tension. And he chose the plot of *I puritani* by proceeding exactly in this manner:

> I leave open the letter addressed to my uncle,[19] so that you can read it and gain an idea of the subject that I will set for the new Paris opera; to you I repeat that I am very happy. A profound interest, events that arrest the soul and invite it to sigh for the suffering innocents, with no evil character who causes these misfortunes; destiny is the one creator, and thereforethe emotions are all the stronger, because there is no human agent to turn to in order to make the misfortunes cease.
>
> My subject is of this type, and I have great hopes that, first, it will inspire me and, second, that it will make a profound impression when united with my melancholic muse.[20]

Bellini chose the plot of the *pièce* by Ancelot (which recalls certain central episodes from *Old Mortality*, the Walter Scott novel published in Italy under the title *I puritani di Scozia*)[21] because its "situations," though extremely sentimental, unfold in an atmosphere of distant fable, far removed from the tensions of a real drama. And the tradition to which this plot relates is again explained by the composer himself: "I swear to you that if the libretto is not capable of [arousing] profound sensations, it is nevertheless full of theatrical effects through its atmosphere; at base it is of a type with *La sonnambula* or Paisiello's *Nina*, with the addition of military robustness and something severely Puritan."[22]

Bellini was therefore aware of the plot's fundamental tone of fable, and he looked at it with a detached eye: "subjective" participation in the emotions and feelings of the characters, such as we find in typically Romantic artists, is completely absent. Not by chance, therefore, did the composer refer to *La sonnambula* as the immediate antecedent of his final opera and to Paisiello's *La Nina pazza per amore* as a remote archetype, an examplar of the unbroken tradition from which his conception of musical theater derived.

It is also worth noting Bellini's continual worry over the reactions of the audience. The choice of plot, the structure of the libretto and thus the articulation of the entire opera, the language to be employed in the realization of the vocal lines—all these were decided with the public's reactions in mind. The necessity of direct communication at the emotional level, or rather in the sphere of several, well-defined emotions, created the need for absolute clarity in establishing the verbal discourse, even before the musical discourse was essayed. And it was here that difficulties arose with Pepoli, who, as a skillful literary figure (one especially inclined toward metrical subtleties), had sought to impose on Bellini his personal view of poetry. We do not, of course, have direct evidence of these discussions, but we can easily deduce them from letters such as the following, which Bellini sent his "poet" near the beginning of their collaboration:

> Carve in your head in adamantine letters: *The "dramma per musica"* [i.e., opera] *must draw tears, terrify people, make them die, through song.* It is wrong to attempt to make all the pieces proceed equally, but they must all in a certain sense be molded so that the music is intelligible by the clarity of their expression: concise and *striking.* Musical artifice kills the effect of the situations, still worse is poetic artifice in a drama for music; poetry and music, in order to make an effect, require naturalness and nothing more; whoever departs from it [i.e., naturalness] is lost, and in the end will give birth to a ponderous, stupid opera that will please only the pedants, never the heart, the poet who receives first the impression of the passions; and, if the heart is moved, one will always be right, even in the face of many, many worthless words.[23]

To conquer his public, Bellini knew no other weapons than to move their feelings, arouse their emotions; and *melodramma* is nothing more than a sequence of fixed emotional situations, clearly designed in their psychological-sentimental aspect, each exactly enclosed within the orbit of the situation, to which a similarly well-defined, self-enclosed form corresponds at the musical level.

We must return for a moment to the composer's (and his favorite librettist, Romani's) attitude toward the singers and toward the fundamental influence this attitude had over the music. The conception of an opera as an articulated unity of parts, differentiated but not necessarily contrasting, and the position of the composer toward the vocal interpreters are at base complementary; each is at once the cause and the effect of the other. This state of affairs is reflected directly in the compositional process. It is significant that we do not possess—nor have we any knowledge of—Bellini sketches that embrace the entire opera; there are merely fragments of sketches, sheets of paper containing melodies annotated by the composer *before* the conception of the opera and used at a later stage once the place, the "situation" appropriate to them, had been found.[24]

This method of conceiving the music corresponds to the basic structure of *melodramma* and influences its overall organization. If one had to alter the emotional "color," or even if one wished to exert a specific effect on the audience, a passage or scene could easily be transported from one point in the plot to another, in spite of the risk of losing verisimilitude or even credibility. Occasions of this type occurred from the very beginning of work on *I puritani*. On 30 May 1834 Bellini wrote to Pepoli: "Today I hope to orchestrate the Introduzione; but I wonder whether the *Inno di Guerra* is superfluous, and think I might place it in the body of the opera, if the situation demands it, if it is truly superfluous where it now stands, since I have rightly made a principal chorus of '*Quando la tromba squilla*,' etc."[25]

THE STORY of this *Inno di guerra* is typical of Bellini's compositional technique. The chorus, that was in part intended to represent that "military robustness" that the composer mentioned to Florimo,[26] had been inserted by Pepoli into the unfolding of the action and mirrored his patriotic sentiments; it was, however, basically foreign to the musico-dramatic conception and also to Bellini's personal ideals.[27] Because the chorus "Quando la tromba squilla" had in the meantime been developed, and since the two pieces were to have exactly the same character, the *Inno di Guerra* had to be moved. In letters that immediately follow the one cited above, Bellini does not mention the piece. It resurfaces, however, in a letter to Florimo dated 21 September: in the complete scheme of the opera, the "Coro dell'alba o libertà, etc."[28] is the fourth piece in the second act; it thus comes after the "trio for two basses and Grisi," the section that in the definitive version of the opera will become Elvira's grand "Madness aria," "Qui la voce sua soave," accompanied by the "two basses." Again in the letter to Florimo of 21 September, Bellini stated that "the coro di Libertà is composed," while he still had to "write completely the duet [between the two "basses"] and the trio"; these sections would, he proposed, be finished last, after the solo and choral parts had been completed.[29] (We might note in passing that these criteria about the order of composition had just received the approval of Rossini.[30]) But as early as 10 October Bellini, unable to tolerate a chorus that he felt was a basic intrusion into the formal and emotional equilibrium of the opera, wrote to Florimo: "[. . .] I see now that [in the libretto] there will be nothing immoral or political: there is just a chorus, that Pepoli wanted to slip in, and that I will take out completely or make him change the words, and it's the one whose words I sent you, that was in the 1st act and that now he wants to put in the 2nd (that of the *Alba*, etc.)".[31]

At this stage of composition it seems that Bellini had set aside the idea of inserting the chorus at some unspecified point in the action, or rather that he had rejected the patriotic "situation" that it realized. Yet this was not to be. Once the time came to set to music the "duet for the two basses," during the final stage of compositional activity, the idea—above all, the "situation" that the chorus represented—again took center stage. Describing to Florimo on 21 December the performers' reaction to the music he had just finished, Bellini wrote: "Tamburrini and Lablache [the two "basses"] will have little in the 2nd act; as soloists they can sing only a duet with choral forces, which I will not send to Naples, first because Porto and Pedrazzi would not be able to manage it, and second because it involves love of both country and liberty, etc., etc., thus Tamburrini and Lablache will sulk about the 2nd act, but what can I do?"[32]

What had happened? The duet that the composer had reserved to be set to music last has now become a "duet with choral forces": there has been, in other words, an osmosis of "situations"; the "military robustness" that was to have been realized in the chorus was transferred to the final part of the duet. The "choral forces" were not, after all, put entirely aside, but their function had become marginal: they now accompany, no longer have a soloistic function. The "situation" that was initially to take shape in the *Inno di guerra* (or the "Coro dell'*Alba o libertà*") became the final stretta of the duet, perhaps the most celebrated section in the entire opera: "Suoni la tromba, e intrepido." And, as final proof of the osmosis between the two "parts" of the opera, the duet, which in the complete plan of the opera—set out on 21 September to Florimo—was the second number in Act II, now became the fourth number, that assigned in the plan to the "Coro dell'*Alba o libertà*." In any event, words from this missing chorus even turn up in the Stretta—words, we might note, that make no sense in the new "situation" and that appear only in the score, not in printed libretti of early performances of *I puritani* in Italy:

> Suoni la tromba, e intrepido
> Io pugnerò da forte,
> Bello è affrontar la morte
> Gridando libertà.
> *All'alba*!
>
> [Sound the trumpet, and fearless
> I will fight to the last,
> It is fine to greet death
> With cries of liberty.
> *To the dawn*!]

On 5 January 1835 the idea of a separate chorus was finally eliminated, or at least work on the duet was very near the final version: "I am still working on the duet for the two basses, which is frightfully *liberal*, and then I must, indeed I want to do an overture [. . .]."[33]

A little before the first performance (on 25 January 1835) Bellini was still working on the duet and enjoined Pepoli to help by appealing (with little or no personal involvement, as we can deduce from his confidential words to Florimo) to his collaborator's patriotic sentiments: "[. . .] I need you to adjust some verses in the duet that I have almost finished; it is magnificent, and the blare of the trumpets will make liberal hearts in the theater tremble with joy [. . .]."[34]

In terms of effect, Bellini was absolutely correct: from the first perfomance onward the composer's prediction came to pass exactly:

> 2nd act (we have divided the opera into three acts, putting Grisi's aria ["Ah, rendetemi la speme"] before the duet for the two basses: and after [we have put] this piece, that closes the 2nd act, because there is no greater effect than what is aroused by that duet) [. . .]. I can say nothing more of the effect made by the two basses. The French all went mad, made such a noise, such cries, that they themselves were amazed to be so transported; but they say that the Stretta of that piece attacks everyone's nerves, and it's true, because with the effect of that Stretta the entire stalls rose to their feet, shouting, then stopping themselves, then shouting again [. . .].[35]

The "situations," each taken separately and then realized in well-differentiated musical sections, were the basis on which Bellini built his musical theater, the mosaic of his operatic discourse. The voices of the soloists have a decisive role both in the overall economy of the opera and in the single numbers given to them. However, in order to move the audience's emotions, Bellini used several devices to place the expressive potential of a character in greater relief. With the exception of Riccardo's first-act aria, "Ah, per sempre io ti perdei," none of the vocal episodes in *I puritani* is given *exclusively* to one voice: the soloist, especially in the closing sections of single verses, is joined by one or more of the other characters on stage, or by the chorus, or by both. Moreover, though there is no need to develop the point here, it is worth stressing that this complexity at the vocal level corresponds to a complexity (also relative and functional but nonetheless very noticeable) at the harmonic and orchestral levels.

The idea of musical theater organized as a series of distinct "situations" through which the vocal virtuosity of the performers can appeal, above all emotionally, to the public is not of course unique to Bellini's poetics. But no other composer illustrated this stylistic choice in such detail and with such clarity of conception; and in Bellini's musical realization it acquires an unmistakeable physiognomy.

Furthermore, there are other moments in *I puritani* that, in my opinion, anticipate new horizons and interests, that tend toward aims broader than that of simple emotional effect on the spectator. We should not forget the functionality of this emotional effect: for the composer, it was the most immediate and direct means of obtaining success with the public.

In this opera Bellini became aware of the physical ambience, of the space within which his characters live and move and the "situations" unfold. Musical realization of this space was certainly not unknown in the operas that precede *I puritani*: one recalls the opening chorus of *Il pirata*, with its echo effects intended to create precisely that sense of "distance," and thus of space. Indeed, the need to characterize musically the physical ambience had already caused some telling moments; for instance, at the beginning of *La sonnambula*, with the placement of the chorus onstage and the use of an offstage banda; or in the first act of *Norma*, where once more the offstage banda and chorus strikingly depict the dimensions of the Druids' forest. However, the complexity of the spatial definition in the opening scene of *I puritani* is unique. The starting point was Pepoli's stage direction: "Spacious embankment of the fortress. Various defenses, towers, and other works of fortification with drawbridges, etc., are to be seen. In the distance are seen very picturesque mountains, which make a most beautiful and solemn view, while the rising sun gradually illuminates them and then brightens the entire scene. On the bastions the sentries are being changed."

If we think again of the librettist's lack of theatrical experience, and of the nature of his collaboration with the composer, it is certainly plausible, keeping in mind the similarities between this and other opening scenes from Bellini's operas, that the description of the physical ambience, of the natural and psychological background against which the action takes place, was more the choice of the composer than that of his "poet." After the fortissimo chords, almost a "Toccata avanti il levar della tela," that open the Introduzione, the musical phrase that begins with the "Puritan" fanfare, played on the horns, is repeated with an insistence that far exceeds a simple exposition (this repetition is in fact incomprehensible if one listens to it without considering its scenic function); the musical cell entrusted to the horns creates, in time, the general character of the ambience in which the plot will unfold. Once the "Puritan severity" is established, the musical definition of the ambience through a variety of devices is laid out in a sort of crescendo. First the choral forces—placed offstage in small groups—exchanges isolated calls strongly emphasized by whole measures of rest; the orchestral repetition of the horns' phrase alternates with these sentries' calls, whose intensified dynamic breaks out into the "Allegro sostenuto e marziale." The point of intersection between the two moments is marked through a dialogue of side drums, also placed in various positions and at various distances from the audience; and the choral forces that sing "Quando la tromba squilla" must—on the composer's explicit instruction—be placed "outside, on the stage, near to the footlights." At the end of this chorus, which is of course a first affirmation of "military robustness," another offstage device, announced by the striking of a bell, serves further to define the musical dimension of the ambience: this is the "Preghiera puritana," performed by the soloists and accompanied only by the organ. It stands out distinctly against the gentle dawn background that the preceding sections have so clearly delineated and is framed at the beginning and end by repetitions of and motives from the dialogue between Bruno and the soldiers, who are silent and immobile onstage while it takes place. The following chorus of castle-dwellers—"Allegro brillante" that concludes the Introduzione—itself opens with an offstage anticipation of its motto: the first sopranos' "A festa!"

Additional proof of Bellini's increasing interest in "offstage" effects intended to establish and define the musical space is found in the central part of the first-act duet between Giorgio and Elvira. When Giorgio had narrated to his niece the conversation with her father, and the agreement of the latter to her marriage with Arturo, the bass is interrupted by the reprise of the offstage horn call ("sounds of hunting horns are heard outside the fortress"), and this leads to an exact repetition of the "Puritan" phrase from the Introduzione. This moment represents the confirmation of what Giorgio has been telling his niece: Arturo is coming to join her; but, by our hearing the Puritans' greeting the "brave and noble count" from offstage, the musical dimension acquires powerful evocative force and persuasive energy. In the climactic moment, the turning point of the "situation," Bellini broadens the musical space and exploits it to the maximum in order to stress the shift from doubt and anguished hope to exultant certainty. Analysis of this new Bellinian attitude[36] could continue with a discussion of the beginning of the third act: from the storm to Arturo's recitative, interrupted first by the singing—again offstage—of Elvira, and then by the calls of the soldiers who are pursuing him, a scene of compelling dramatic complexity, articulated with an extraordinary control of colors and "dimensions."

With this chapter I have simply tried to offer certain observations arising from a detailed reading of the score with which Bellini closed his brief career; I have tried at the same time to point out certain directions that the study of nineteenth-century Italian opera could take toward a greater cultural appreciation of this complex artistic phenomenon.

Notes

1. See chapters 1 and 2, and also "Balzac, Stendhal e il *Mosè* di Rossini," in *Annuario 1965–1970* (del Conservatorio di musica "G. B. Martini" di Bologna) (Bologna, 1971), 203–19. English translation in Gioacchino Rossini, *The Barber of Seville/Moses*, English National Opera Guide no. 36 (London and New York, 1985), 99–108. See also Luigi Dallapiccola's "Parole e musica nel melodramma," cited in chap. 1, n. 31.

2. This essay was written in spring 1969; a few months later appeared Friedrich Lippmann's *Vincenzo Bellini und die Italienische Opera seria seiner Zeit—Studien über Libretto, Arienform und Melodik* (*Analecta musicologica*—Veröffentlichungen der Musikabteilung des Deutschen Historischen Instituts in Rom, Band 6) (Cologne and Vienna, 1969). More recently, a much-expanded Italian version of this book has appeared as Maria Rosaria Adamo and Friedrich Lippmann, *Vincenzo Bellini* (Turin, 1981). Lippmann's work discusses for the first time with rigor and enormous thoroughness several aspects of Bellini's work. My thanks to my colleague Dr. Lippmann for the invaluable advice and suggestions he offered me while I was at work on the present study.

3. Francesco Pastura's book *Bellini secondo la storia* (Parma, 1959) only rarely confronts musico-dramatic problems, and more often than not it does so in an impressionistic manner; Ildebrando Pizzetti's "La musica di Vincenzo Bellini," in *La voce* 7 (1915), reprinted in *Intermezzi critici* (Florence, n.d.), 33–112, and in *La musica italiana dell'800* (Turin, 1947), 149–228, although it offers detailed inquiries and interesting musical observations, is ruled in both conception and realization by the author's (rather than his

subject's) poetics; Pizzetti, albeit involuntarily, superimposes on and attributes to Bellini his own conception of musical theater.

Leslie Orrey's monograph, *Bellini* (London, 1969), was the first systematic attempt at musical analysis of the entire Bellinian corpus. Although full of acute observations and impossible to ignore in any future work on the composer, it nevertheless betrays some rather impressionistic critical judgments and also contains a fair number of historical inaccuracies.

4. The best source for Bellini's letters remains Vincenzo Bellini, *Epistolario*, ed. Luisa Cambi (Verona, 1943).

5. See Pastura, 410–11.

6. Bellini, *Epistolario*, 391.

7. According to Pastura, 411, this period saw the birth of the Sapphic ode "Alla luna" and the four sonnets "Amore," "Malinconia," "La ricordanza," and "Speranza," all for voice and piano, set by Bellini to texts by Pepoli. With one exception, neither the text nor the music of these compositions has survived. See Filippo Cicconetti, *Vita di Vincenzo Bellini* (Prato, 1859). The autograph of "La ricordanza" is in the Library of Congress in Washington; see Orrey, 160.

8. Bellini, *Epistolario*, 393.

9. Ibid., 394.

10. In this context, it is interesting to see the importance Bellini attributed to the choice of subject for the libretto. In an undated letter, almost certainly from April 1834, probably addressed to Cav. Galeota, the composer writes: "It is the most difficult thing to find subjects that offer novelty and interest, and it is the only reason that causes so much delay; since I am convinced that the libretto is the foundation of the opera, I have found the time in searching for it well spent" (from ibid., 397).

11. Ibid., 26–27.

12. Ibid., 438–39.

13. Ibid., 439.

14. Ibid., 454–55.

15. Ibid., 401.

16. Ibid., 439.

17. Ibid., 157–58.

18. Letter to Florimo, undated, but from September 1828, during the genesis of *La straniera*; from ibid., 146.

19. This letter, which contains a detailed summary of the plot of *I puritani*, was discovered by Pastura and is published in his book (see n. 3), 412–13.

20. Bellini, *Epistolario*, 395. The letter, dated Paris, 11 April 1834, is addressed to Santocanale.

21. The choice of title for the opera seems to have been made with precisely this coincidence in mind, even though there is no direct connection between the novel and the libretto: "If the title *Puritani* is troublesome, then let it be *Elvira* or *Le teste rotonde ed i Cavalieri*. This last is too long, and we have chosen the first because it is well-known through the *Puritani* of *Valter-Scott* [*sic*]" (from a letter to Florimo dated 21 November 1834; in ibid., 470).

22. Letter to Florimo dated 4 October 1834, which means when the composition of *I puritani* was well advanced; from ibid., 442. There are at least five further direct refer-

ences in Bellini's *Epistolario* (pp. 429, 452, 455, 486, 487) to the resemblances in subject matter and situation to Paisiello's opera; see also chapter 11.

23. Undated letter to Pepoli (but from May 1834); see Bellini, *Epistolario*, 400.

24. See, for example, the facsimile reproduction of autograph pages housed in the Museo Belliniano of Catania, reproduced in Pastura (see n. 3), opposite pp. 385 and 400. See also the letter to Lamperi dated 14 June 1834: "I have nothing new: only that I have composed four pieces and that I am always pounding my head to find those little motives that now seem rare in Europe" (see ibid., 404–5).

25. Ibid., 403.

26. See the letter dated 4 October 1834, cited above in n. 22.

27. See the letter to Florimo dated 26 May 1834: "This hymn is done solely for Paris, where they like thoughts of liberty. You understand? For Italy Pepoli will himself change the entire hymn and will not even mention the word *libertà* [freedom], and he will also change any liberal phrases in the opera; thus there's no need to worry, because the libretto will be put straight, if they want to perform the opera in Naples"; see Bellini, *Epistolario*, 401.

28. That this chorus corresponds to the *Inno di Guerra* can be deduced from a note by Florimo, who, in reporting the text of the Bellini letter sent to him on 26 May 1834, gives the following précis of this point in the opera: "Here one recalls the plot of *I puritani*, and transcribes the poetry of the Introduzione, from the words "All'erta" to the words "All'alba sorgerà—Il sol di libertà." From *Bellini—Memorie e lettere*, ed. Francesco Florimo (Florence, 1882), 413.

29. "If tomorrow you will have ready the duet *il cor dell'alba* and then immediately work *on the finale*, I'll be much obliged, since I soon want to write out what I have already composed, in order then to think about creating the duet for the two basses, and the trio; pieces that I will do last, after having completed the rest" (letter to Pepoli dated 19 September 1834; from Bellini, *Epistolario*, 433).

30. "I have told all this to Rossini, as if to ask advice of him, and he replied that I do well to finish everything else first and then compose the two aforementioned pieces"; from ibid., 439.

31. Ibid., 452.

32. Ibid., 492.

33. Letter to Florimo; from ibid., 489.

34. Ibid., 499.

35. Letter to Florimo dated 26 January 1835; from ibid., 501.

36. A significant example, which Bellini must have studied closely for the problem of the expressive effect of offstage devices, can be found in the Act II finale of *Guillaume Tell*, the "giuramento" scene.

CHAPTER 11

BELLINI AND PAISIELLO: FURTHER DOCUMENTS ON THE BIRTH OF *I PURITANI*

THE CREATION OF a work of art may sometimes remain mysterious because of lack of information on the compositional act that gave it birth. When documents exist, however, they can illuminate the various phases through which the opera took its final shape: the basic criteria, the working method, the ideas and decisions that the author established during the creative act. But a document concerned with the composing process can also shed light, if only indirectly, on the larger significance of a work and on its exact historical position. It is easier that all this happens when the artist is constrained by external circumstances to break the silence of his *modus operandi*, a silence allowed him by his use of accepted, commonly understood conventions, whose guidelines he had until then been content to follow. This is precisely the case with Bellini. For none of his operas does such rich documentation exist as for *I puritani*—because of the level of commitment it drew from him (the opera was to be his official debut on the Parisian stage), but even more because he was no longer collaborating with Felice Romani (with whom he had had a falling out). His new collaborator, Count Pepoli, was entirely without experience in writing texts for music, and those for theatrical music; this obliged the composer repeatedly to expound and clarify—in writing—the basic criteria of the work they shared as well as to discuss the successes achieved and the problems still to be overcome in letters to his Neapolitan friend Francesco Florimo.

I have addressed these matters before[1] and would perhaps not have returned to them were it not for the kindness and generosity of Andrew Porter, who put at my disposal a further document, until now almost completely unknown to Bellini scholars, which contains new information on the birth of *I puritani*. To understand and evaluate precisely the importance of this document, we need to review the circumstances that surrounded its origin.

Bellini arrived in Paris from London at the end of summer 1833. Commissioned to write a new opera for the Théâtre Italien, to be performed by the end of 1834, he did not start work before February of that year. It was during this period, and in the salon of Cristina Trivulzio Belgiojoso, that he made the acquaintance of an aristocratic Bolognese, Carlo Pepoli, who had been exiled for the part he had played in the 1831 uprisings in Romagna. Pepoli was in Paris mainly to cure an eye disease that he had contracted in a Venetian prison, where he had been incarcerated after having been captured by the Austrians while fleeing by ship following the failure of the uprising.[2] At least at first, the collaboration suited both partners; they set about choosing a subject for the new opera. The criteria that governed this choice were clear and precise: they needed to find, according to Bellini, "subjects that present novelty and interest"[3] not only to the composer but also (indeed, above all) to the public; and the plot must be something that the public already knew and was sympathetic toward[4]—it was usually a spoken drama at that moment enjoying great success.[5]

Once the choice was made, Pepoli and Bellini had to extract from the theatrical model the various "situations," the moments in the plot that would correspond to the "numbers" of the score. Each "situation" would form the basis of a section of the opera; and each section was conceived as a musical definition of the "affect" that characterized and distinguished the situation.[6] The librettist then strove to define this "affect" in the manner most suitable for the composer and singer—by choosing words and rhythms that were easy to sing.[7] In this type of work Felice Romani was the ideal collaborator: he was in command of a poetic technique completely attuned to the musical intentions of the composer, and he was also capable of guiding the composer in singling out "situations" from the original play.[8] Pepoli, on the other hand, was the opposite: this was his first experience as a librettist, and Bellini was obliged to take charge of the enterprise himself.[9] This situation gave rise to uncertainties over the order of the pieces and to various reshufflings that became necessary as the work developed. It was at this delicate and important phase—the move from spoken drama to libretto—that we find the document to be discussed for the first time in the following pages; and it is thanks to this kind of information that we can identify both the sources and the models that were referred to and the manner in which the creative act took place.

The first performance of *Têtes rondes et Cavaliers*, the play Pepoli and Bellini chose for their opera, preceded by only a few months their decision to use this spoken drama as the basis for the libretto.[10] The adaptation began, naturally, with the first act; a letter from Bellini to his uncle Francesco Ferlito in Catania, dated 11 April 1834, contains a fairly detailed précis of the action in the first act of both the play and the opera.[11] In this act the only important point of divergence from the spoken drama is the scene with which the score begins. Although the play calls for an internal stage set, the "grand salle de la forteresse" held by the Puritans, the first scene of the opera takes place outdoors, on the bastions; and the sense of a broad open space was created by Bellini through exclusively musical means. As Massimo Mila stressed with characteristic acuteness, "In this opera [. . .] it is no exaggeration to say that the ambience is the true protagonist, the constant source of life and artistic truth."[12]

The transition from play to libretto was, however, rather more difficult in the rest of the opera. At one point the decision was made to have only two acts,[13] and up to a few days before the first performance various changes in the order of pieces and other significant alterations were still taking place.[14] All these structural problems are revealed extensively by the composer's correspondence during the second half of 1834. However, what was clear to Bellini from the very beginning was the fundamental character of the opera, which he intended to bring to life with precise musical means:

> A profound interest, events that arrest the soul and invite it to sigh for the suffering innocents, with no evil character who causes these misfortunes; destiny is the one creator, and therefore the emotions are all the stronger because there is no human agent to turn to in order to make the misfortunes cease.
>
> My subject is of this type, and I have great hopes that, first, it will inspire me and, second, that it will make a profound impression when united with my melancholic muse.[15]

The spoken drama contains characters and scenes that have nothing to do with this precisely defined *tinta*—consider for example Sara and the Puritan Habacuc, or the comic scenes. Nor should one forget that in deciding on the succession of pieces, Bellini needed to parcel out the singers' roles equally, to satisfy their various demands. In the move from play to libretto, therefore, the irrelevant had to be eliminated and the chosen elements organized in an effective manner, so that their form and scoring could then be decided upon. In this way Bellini invented musical "situations" and numbers, though he was ready to change their function and order as the work evolved.

TWO DOCUMENTS, of exactly the same general type and fairly similar in content, bear witness to this moment in the creative act: they are both in the composer's hand, and both sketch out the "situations" and succession of musical pieces in the second and third acts of the opera. As explained by a note of authentication Pepoli added to one of them when he decided to give it to a lady friend, both documents are in Bellini's hand because the "poet" could not write owing to his eye disorder. In my opinion, the earlier of them is the one published—with some dubious readings and omissions—by Bellini's biographer, Francesco Pastura;[16] the original is now in the Astor Lenox Tilden Foundation collection of the Library and Museum of the Performing Arts in New York,[17] and is transcribed again here not only to clarify the discussion but also because a more accurate transcription reveals the various phases in which it was written. An initial phase follows step by step the order of the play, which Bellini evidently had at hand. Sometime later, the composer marked the succession of scenes and added in the margin what he imagined as the "numbers" of the score, indicating the musical form and the characters that appear; a sort of bracket placed at the side of the text encloses precisely that section of the plot that will correspond to the "number."[18] A third phase of elaboration is revealed by the crossing-out with oblique pen-strokes of the text originally conceived as the second "number," the grand "Scena [di] Elvira" (Elvira's scene); Bellini decided to replace it with "Qualche altra cosa invece—forse un coro" (something else—perhaps a chorus); this phrase is thus written above the cancellation and between the line of the previous text (plate 11.1).[19]

2nd Act. Scene as in the *play* Act I

1st, 2nd, and 3rd scenes of the play will form the trio, etc.

Giorgio pauses to wipe away a tear. Recit: Ah! je ne puis pas voir cela... Dire qu'il y a des moments ou elle ne me reconna[isse] même pas! [Ah! I cannot look at that . . . To say that there are moments when she does not even recognize me!] etc., etc. Scene 2 Mulgrave comes onstage Recit still with Giorgio until Elvira's Romanza is heard. Scene 3 after [she] comes onstage there comes the trio Elvira-Giorgio-Mulgrave. The last will have the principal part in this piece. Scene 4 Elvira remains alone. *Grand scene in the middle of which an offstage chorus, of sentries, or peasants, according to which seems better in the situation, of a type similar to the voice of the gondolier that Desdemona hears in the moment of her misfortune, etc., etc. After that scene comes Giorgio.* Scene 5 Duettino of the dance, etc., etc. Perhaps instead of the dance Elvira will oblige her uncle to repeat the lines of the Romanza or another passage with a cheerful character, etc., etc.——

Scene 6 The scene must be changed if possible, etc., etc. Storm etc., Clifford Recit. Duet with Giorgio [underneath: main part] that ends as a trio with scene 7 etc., etc. Giorgio leaves

Finale

Recit. and duet Elvira and Clifford made up of Scenes 8, 9, 10, and 11 *of the play*, taking out the useless tutti in scene 12.

3rd Act

Chorus of conspirators
Recit. and duet Giorgio and Elvira
Recit. and duet Mulgrave and Clifford
Finale.[20]

The precise references to scenes in the play, and especially the direct quotation of the sentence that opens the second act of *Têtes rondes et Cavaliers*,[21] are proof that this document reflects a fairly early stage of work on the opera. But the characters of Sara and Habacuc have already been eliminated, replaced by

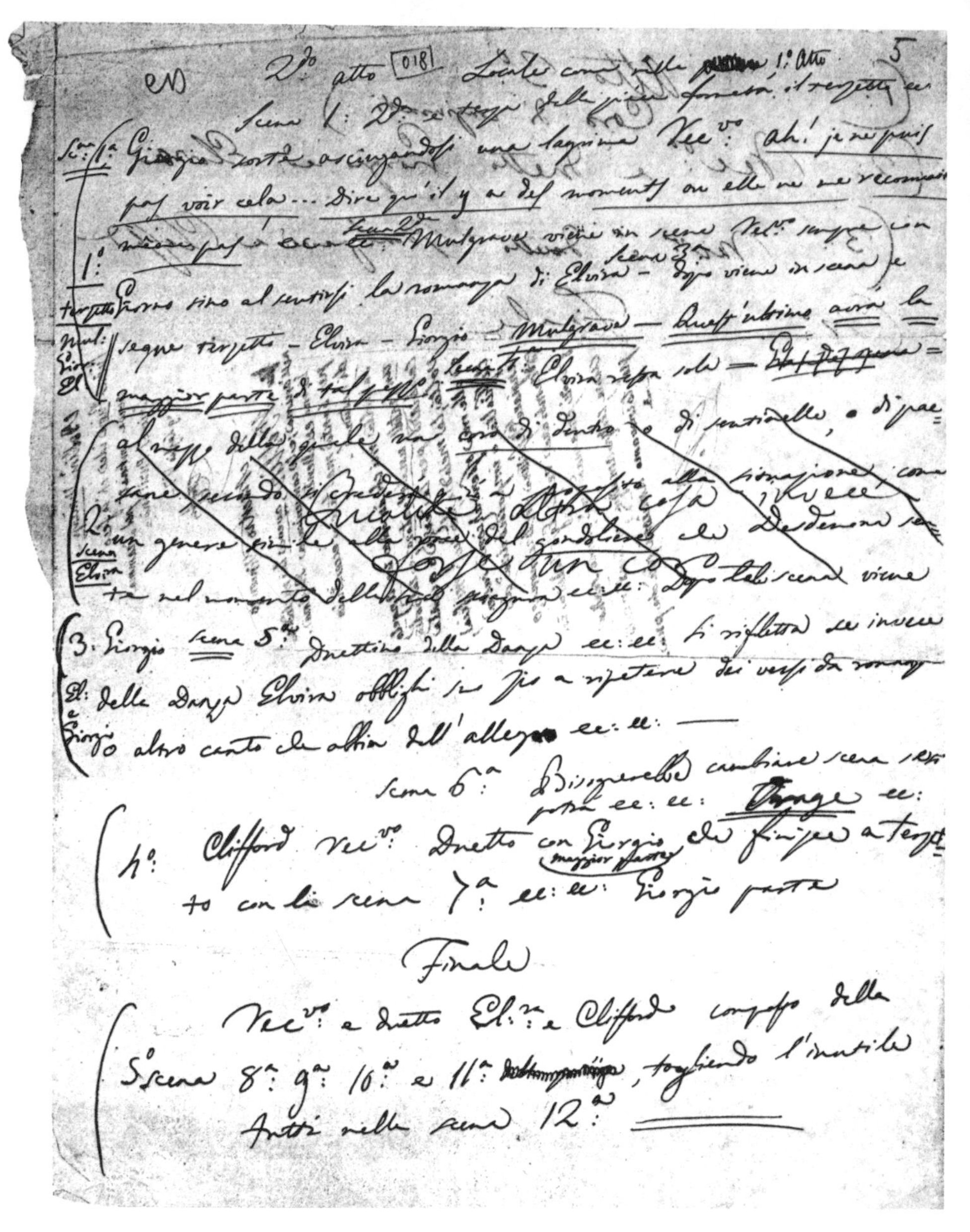

Plate 11.1. Bellini, early sketches for the libretto of Acts II and III of *I puritani*, recto (Astor Lenox Tilden Foundation Collection, Library and Museum of the Performing Arts, New York)

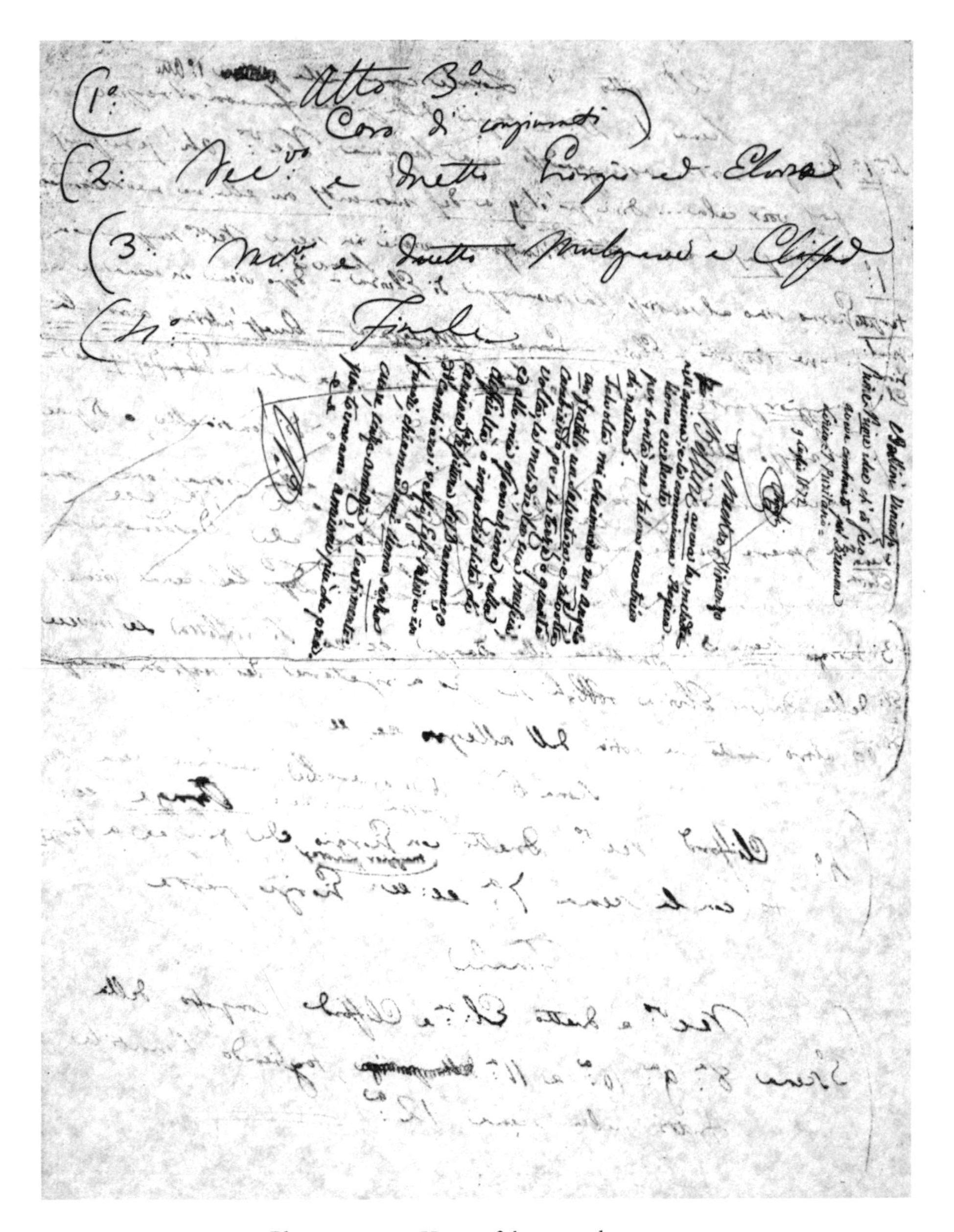

1° Atto 3°
Coro di congiurati
2. Rec.vo e Duetto Giorgio ed Elvira
3. Rec.vo e Duetto Mulgrave e Clifford
4°. Finale

Plate 11.1, *cont.* Verso of the same document

Giorgio: he is given the words cited at the beginning of the text. The scene in which a distracted Lucy forces the puritan Habacuc to dance with her[22] is transformed into the "duettino della danza" between Elvira and Giorgio. Bellini does not exclude the idea of eliminating the dance entirely, fashioning things so that "Elvira will oblige her uncle to repeat the lines of the Romanza or another passage with a cheerful character," a clear indication of the composer's tendency to entrust the expression to voices rather than instruments. The final part of the second act—from the fourth "number" of the score and sixth scene of the play onward—is already conceived as a self-contained entity, to the extent that Bellini even asked for a change of scene; it contains in embryo what will become the first part of the third act in the opera's final version.

This document is also relevant from another point of view. In the section of the sketch that corresponds to the fourth scene of the play—a section Bellini first marked as a grand scene for Elvira and which he later wanted to replace "perhaps" with a chorus—the function of the chorus "of sentries, or peasant girls" is made clear by the explicit reference to a compositional model, "of a type similar to the voice of the *gondolier* that Desdemona hears in the moment of her misfortune."[23] The reference to Rossini's *Otello* was undoubtedly suggested by the similarity of the two "situations": in both a single voice—or a chorus—echoes offstage, at the climactic moment of the plot, the sentiments of a young woman, the innocent victim of cruel destiny.

It is important to realize that even though Bellini had a very clear idea of the models and archetypes to which he could turn, he looked to them not for direct citations or textual references but in order to shape his personal theatrical language by following their example. In this sense, some unique evidence is offered by the other sketch for Acts II and III of *I puritani* .[24] In this manuscript Bellini's handwriting is much more relaxed than in the New York sketch and with only two exceptions—the note added on the side of the folio and the crossing-out of Clifford's (= Arturo's) aria in the third act—the text seems to have been written without second thoughts or revisions (plate 11.2).

2nd Act

Int[roduzio]ne (Introduction) Chorus of household members = they deplore the fate of Eloisa; at the appearance of the Uncle they turn to him and ask for news. Here Recit. and then he [= the Uncle] will start an aria with <u>many words</u>, which explains all the details of his Niece's madness, and what she thinks she sees in the worst stages of her illness.(1)

[to the side, on the margin of the folio]

(1) The Uncle orders the chorus to have the peasant girls come and gather flowers, etc., etc. and try to distract Eloisa, etc.

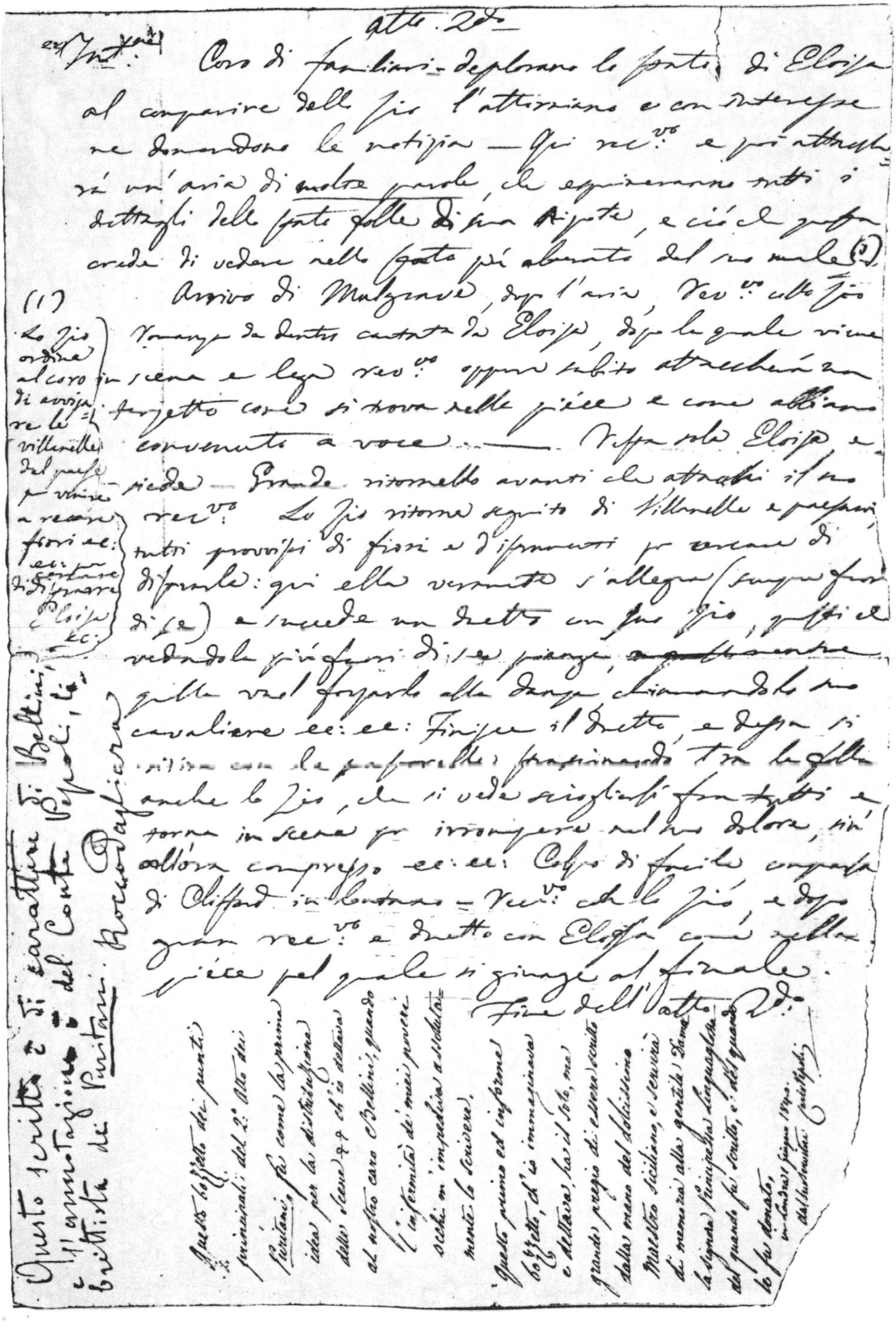

Plate 11.2. Bellini, later libretto sketches for Acts II and III of *I puritani* (private collection of Andrew Porter, London)

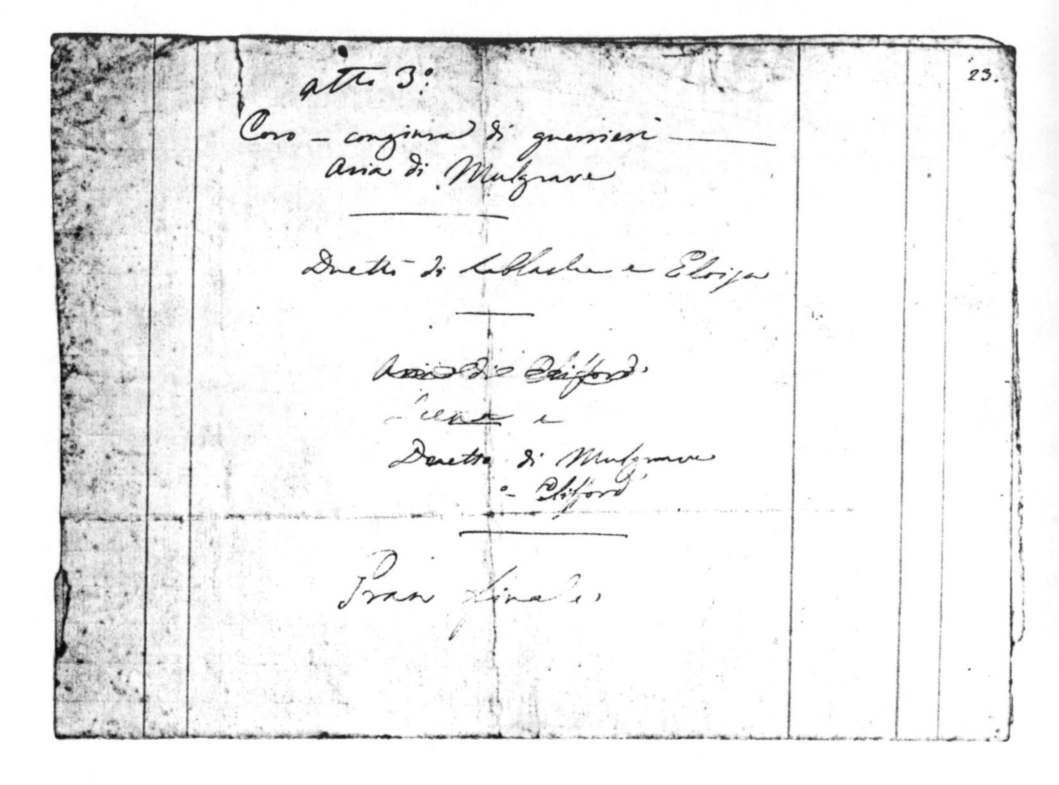

23.

atto 3°

Coro – congiura di guerrieri
Aria di Mulgrave

Duetto di Lablache e Eloisa

Aria di Clifford
Scena e
Duetto di Mulgrave
e Clifford

Gran Finale

Plate 11.2, *cont.* Verso of the same document

Arrival of Mulgrave, after the aria, Recit. with the Uncle. Offstage Romanza sung by Eloisa, after which she comes onstage and begins without a break a Recit. or immediately begins a trio such as is found in the play and as we have agreed in conversation.——Eloisa remains alone and sits down. Grand refrain before she begins her Recit. The Uncle returns followed by the Peasant girls and men, all with flowers and instruments in order to distract her: here she truly becomes happy (though still beside herself) and there follows a duet with her Uncle, who weeps to see her thus distracted, *and she invites* [?] while she tries to force him to dance, calling him her cavalier, etc., etc. The duet ends, and she retires with the shepherdesses, dragging with her into the crowd her Uncle, whom we see disengage himself and return onstage to burst out with sorrow, which until now he has held back, etc., etc. A gunshot, Clifford appears in the distance. —Recit. with the Uncle, and afterwards a grand Recit. and duet with Eloisa as in the play, and with which the finale is reached.

End of 2nd Act

3rd Act

Chorus—warriors' conspiracy
Mulgrave's Aria

Duet between Lablache and Eloisa

Clifford's Aria
Scene and
Duet for Mulgrave and Clifford

Grand Finale[25]

With the exception of the "Mulgrave's Aria" and an immediately canceled attempt at alteration (Clifford's Aria), Bellini repeats for the third act the scheme he laid out in the New York sketch. This scheme will be so different in the definitive score as to be almost unrecognizable. Already in this second sketch the protagonist's name is no longer Elvira (a name that will be restored in the definitive version) but Eloisa. However, the most interesting and surprising modifications occur at the beginning of the second act where, instead of a simple recitative for Giorgio, there are plans for an Introduzione: a choral section, a sort of dialogue between the chorus and Giorgio, and finally an aria for Giorgio ("with many words"), in which he describes his niece's madness. The archetype toward which Bellini gestured for this new scene—and for the remainder of the act—is, even if not explicitly stated, unmistakable: it is Paisiello's *La Nina ossia la pazza per amore*. Once again it was the close similarity of dramatic situation that prescribed the model. The opening scene of Paisiello's opera takes place in a garden where Nina, mad for love of her Lindoro, is sleeping. A chorus "di Villani e di Villane" (of peasant men and women) exchange words with Giorgio "balio del Conte" (tutor to the Count) and Nina's father, and with Elisa "governante di Nina" (Nina's governess)[26] lamenting the fate of her "padroncina" (little mistress). The new name of Bellini's protagonist is clearly modeled on that of the governess, while the "balio" (tutor), together with "Georges Monk," "general du Parlement" in the Ancelot and Xavier play, lends his name to the uncle of Lucy-Eloisa-Elvira. But the principal lesson Bellini drew from Paisiello's opera lies in the structure of the scene, one that—significantly—will undergo no later changes and will remain at that precise place in the score, exactly as sketched during this phase of the creative process. In a letter to Pepoli simply dated "Friday morning" (which, according to the editor of Bellini's correspondence, "is usually dated 8 September 1834"[27]), the composer gave his librettist detailed instructions on how to develop the dialogue between Giorgio and the chorus, following the directions given in our sketch:

> As for the chorus that opens the second part, I think it's rather short; so try to make it eight lines,[28] and try to do a chorus that is worthy of the lines that Giorgio says [. . .]. One more little thing about the chorus. —Coro. Qual novella? G. Or prende posa. Coro[.] miserella! è insana ognor?— [Chorus: What news? G: Now she is resting. Chorus: Poor girl! Is she still mad?]. Here instead of beginning "Cinta di rose, etc." [Garlanded with roses] I should like Giorgio to reply "Ah! sì ognor" [Ah! yes, always] (for example). The chorus, "senza tregua?" [no relief?]. Giorgio then says: "Accostatevi, ascoltate" [Gather round, listen] (for example), or something similar, etc., etc.
>
> In this way the scene will be prepared, and attention will be focused with greater intensity on the start of the narrative.[29]

This amplification is again directly modeled on the opening scene of *Nina*, in which the "Peasants" beg Giorgio and Elisa to narrate how the young girl became mad. In fact, Andrew Porter's sketch allows us to see how, completely taken up with the model at hand, Bellini ran the risk of forgetting that his plot was set in an English castle in the middle of the seventeenth century. He wanted Giorgio to order the chorus to "have the peasant girls [from the village] come and gather flowers [. . .] and try to distract Eloisa"; later on, Giorgio returns onstage "followed by the Peasant girls and men, all with flowers and instruments in order to distract her," and at the end of the duet between Eloisa and Giorgio the young madwoman "retires with the shepherdesses." The "puritan severity" and "robust military atmosphere" that, according to Bellini, were essential features of his score[30] were in danger of being overwhelmed by the rustic and *larmoyant* tone that permeates Marsollier's comedy and Paisiello's opera.

THE LETTER to Pepoli from which I quoted earlier begins: "The trio is fine as you have arranged it." Bellini had already voiced his approval of this text when writing to Florimo four days earlier, saying that the librettist had written "a very beautiful trio between the two Basses and Grisi, as interesting as the quartet in *Nina*."[31] This trio, if I am not mistaken, corresponds to the first musical "number" of the sketch now in New York and to the "trio such as is found in the play and as we have agreed in conversation" in the Andrew Porter sketch. However, in moving from one sketch to the other, and under the influence of Paisiello, the trio changed position and character. In the first sketch the principal voice in the "number" was that of Mulgrave (one of the "two Basses," the character who will become Riccardo in the definitive version of the opera): "Mulgrave—The last will have the principal part in this piece," and the trio is located at the beginning of the act. In the second sketch the trio is replaced at the beginning by the Introduzione, Giorgio's dialogue with the chorus and his Romanza; one could not, of course, have two adjacent numbers featuring a bass voice. Therefore, some weeks later, on 21 September, after having announced to Florimo that "I have orchestrated everything in the 2nd act that I have put down on paper, which is a coro d'introduzione (introductory chorus) with a Romanza for Lablache,[32] a description of his niece's madness [. . .],"[33] Bellini informed his Neapolitan friend that the trio was now the third "number" in Act II. And he explained the change of place and disposition of voices in these significant terms:

> 3rd Trio for two basses and Grisi[34]
> this is like the quartet from *Nina*, in which the female role has everything; it will, then, seem almost like a solo scene for her.[35]

From a similarity of dramatic situation we have moved to a more specific musical correspondence. About a month later, again writing to Florimo, Bellini confirmed the relationship with the "number" that closes the first act of Paisiello's opera:

> You tell me to finish the opera *I puritani* with a grand scene for the woman; this was my intention; but because of very sensible alterations made to the 2nd act, the scene for the woman falls in the center of the act, a situation which in some ways resembles the quartet from *Nina*; but with a different atmosphere ("altro colorito") because there is melancholy, then joy, then something indeterminate, and it closes with an agitated forte: the two basses will play secondary vocal roles ("gli faranno da pertichini") [. . .].[36]

Gradually the trio became Elvira's grand aria, "Ah, rendetemi la speme"—and it did so without too much expenditure of musical energy, given that on 19 September Bellini wrote to Pepoli:

> If tomorrow you will prepare for me the duet "*il cor dell'alba*," and then immediately work on *the finale*, I will be very much obliged, since I should like soon to write out [in full] what I have already composed, in order to move on to the creation of the duet for the two basses, and the trio; pieces that I will do last, after having completed all the rest and given it to the copyist, and then study the above-mentioned two pieces seriously, since I want make them successful.[37]

Bellini made further reference to Paisiello's opera when he wanted to explain to Malibran—via a letter to Florimo—the female protagonist of his new opera. He was particularly anxious that the great singer interpret this role in the first Neapolitan performances: "Malibran's part will be extremely interesting because it is the same type as *Nina pazza*; and it has harrowing emotional situations, but the part as it now stands is high and needs to be transposed and recast with new orchestration; thus there are a few days' work ahead [. . .]"[38] The adaptation of *I puritani* to the new, Neapolitan company of singers occupied Bellini during the last two months of 1834: before, that is, the opera had been completed for its first performance.[39] During this period he again stressed—in a further letter to Florimo—the connections with Paisiello's opera: "Tell her [Malibran] that I will accommodate and adapt *I puritani* to her voice and that she need have no fear of the part; since it is passionate like *Nina*, it would be sufficient to have the situations acted by her in prose [i.e., simply acted, not sung] to excite immense interest: also tell her that I wait and sigh for an opportunity to demonstrate to her the extent of my admiration [. . .]."[40]

From all these references it seems clear that, at least from a certain point onward, Bellini had Paisiello's opera as a term of reference during his creative work. And he did so not merely to derive from it the structure of individual episodes but also (perhaps especially) because he felt, and wanted to encourage, a basic affinity of character, of tone, of *tinta* (to use again that most useful Verdian term) between the two scores, especially in passages that concern the protagonist. In this sense, the Bellini opera that most resembles *I puritani* is *La sonnambula*: there is a deliberate absence of profound conflicts; as a consequence—and precisely because the plot hinges on the characters' fundamental "innocence"—the dramatic language is addressed above all to the spectators' emotional reaction. Again, Bellini's thoughts on the matter were very clear: "I swear to you that if the libretto is not capable of [arousing] profound sensations, it is nevertheless full of theatrical effects through its atmosphere, and I can say that at base it is of a type with *La sonnambula* or Paisiello's *Nina*, with the addition of military robustness and something severely Puritan."[41]

Using as a point of departure a play that was at that moment enjoying great success, and then taking from it what would serve his own musico-dramatic conception, Bellini discovered, at a certain point in the creative process, his cultural roots. And he connected himself to them, made use of them, kept them as a model with a clarity of vision we find only in the true artist. In this way, he succeeded in renewing, even though with a completely different language, a type of late eighteenth-century musical theater in which the French and Italian cultures had, once again, found a point of contact and interaction.

Notes

1. See chapter 10 and also my "'Suoni la tromba, e intrepido': dal libretto di Carlo Pepoli per Vincenzo Bellini alle variazioni di Liszt," in *I "Quaderni" de "L'argine"* (Ostiglia, 1974), 9.

2. See Francesco Pastura, *Bellini secondo la storia* (Parma, 1959), 410.

3. Vincenzo Bellini, *Epistolario*, ed. Luisa Cambi (Verona, 1943), 397.

4. "Pepoli has proposed some subjects, and they seem to me interesting. One perhaps for Paris, since it is a French play . . ." (ibid., 393).

5. The same principles will guide the young Verdi in his choice of the *Nabucco* subject: the play by Anicet Bourgeois and Francis-Cornu, first performed in Paris in 1836, had been used as a model for the ballet by Antonio Cortesi, performed at La Scala in 1838. For further details, see chapter 1, 13.

6. For a detailed analysis of this fundamental aspect of Bellini's poetics, see again chapter 10, especially 166–67.

7. "Carve in your head in adamantine letters: *The opera must draw tears, terrify people, make them die, through song*" (Bellini, *Epistolario*, 400).

8. See again chapter 10, again 166–67.

9. "Pepoli has no theatrical experience; I have done what I can to give some form to the set numbers [. . .]" (from a letter to Giovanni Ricordi dated 27 September 1834; in Bellini, *Epistolario*, 440).

10. J.-A.-P.-F. Ancelot and J.X.B. Xavier, *Têtes rondes et Cavaliers*, drame historique en trois actes, mêlé de chant; par MM. Ancelot et Xavier. Representé pour la première fois à Paris, sur le Théâtre National du Vaudeville, le 25 septembre 1833. Paris, 1833.

11. See Pastura, *Bellini*, 412–13.

12. Massimo Mila, *Cent'anni di musica moderna* (Milan, 1944), 43–44.

13. "[. . .] there is a dramatically very impressive duet [un duetto di grande situazione] here that I can say is fully worked out, as is the finale that follows and that closes the opera, since I have persuaded Pepoli to do it in two acts [. . .]" (from a letter to Florimo dated 21 September 1834; in Bellini, *Epistolario*, 438).

14. For a reconstruction of the various stages of what eventually became the duet "of the two Basses" that closes the second act of the opera, "Suoni la tromba, e intrepido," see chapter 10, 169–71.

15. From a letter dated 11 April 1834 to Santocanale; in Bellini, *Epistolario*, 395.

16. Pastura, *Bellini*, 418–19.

17. Shelf mark: Music Reserve + MNY. My thanks to Susan T. Sommer, who kindly

sent me a photocopy of this document, thus enabling a more accurate transcription. A facsimile, too small to be easily legible, is published in Tommasino D'Amico, *Come si ascolta l'opera* (n.p., n.d.), 112–13; the autograph was then in the Natale Gallini collection.

18. We can assume that in general these phases followed each other immediately. From the layout of the text in the manuscript we can deduce that Bellini felt the need to indicate the order of the scenes in the play after having dealt with the content of the fourth scene, and so after the words "Dopo tal scena viene Giorgio (After that scene comes Giorgio)."

19. In the transcription, I have reproduced the manuscript's graphic layout and the underscoring (both single and double); the spaced-out phrase is the only one that Bellini underlines twice in the first phase of writing; words in italics were canceled in the third phase.

20. The scheme for the third act is on the verso of the folio. Laid out at right angles to Bellini's text is the following statement in Pepoli's hand:

> Bellini *Vincenzo*. The *very first* ideas that I worked out with him for the Dramma Lirico = I Puritani =
>
> 9 July 1872—C. Pepoli.
>
> Maestro Vincenzo BELLINI *had* melody in his soul; and he could communicate through it in a sovreign manner. A man of extraordinary goodness but somewhat eccentric by nature.
>
> Sometimes he would call me *an angel, a brother, a Saviour*: and sometimes changing for the third or fourth time the melodies, his music, responding to my remarks on the Difficulty or impossibility of changing the layout of the Drama, or altering the verses, He would leap up in fury, calling me a *Man without* heart, without friendship or feeling: then we would again become great friends, more than before. &c. C. P.

21. Ancelot and Xavier, *Têtes rondes*, 28.

22. Ibid., 57–59.

23. The reference in Rossini's *Otello* is to Desdemona's Act III "Recitativo e Romanza." The text of the gondolier's Canzone is a direct quotation from Dante: "Nessun maggior dolore / che ricordarsi del tempo felice / nella miseria" (*Inferno* 5.121–23) and the melody's contour clearly recalls the "Aria del Tasso" sung by Venetian gondoliers. Two versions of the melody of the "Aria," "transcribed" by Tartini in his sonatas for solo violin, are published in Pierluigi Petrobelli, "Tartini and Folk-Music," in *Report of the Tenth Congress (of the International Musicological Society), Ljubljana 1967*, ed. D. Cvetko (Kassel, Basel, and Paris, 1970), 178. See also my "Dante and Italian Music: Three Moments," *Cambridge Opera Journal* 2 (1990): 219–249.

24. The existence of this document was first mentioned in Andrew Porter, "Bellini's Last Opera," *Opera* 11 (1960): 315–22. On p. 318 Porter remarks: "At least two drafts for the scenario have survived. Pastura in his recent volume transcribes one and I have recently acquired another, earlier one, in Bellini's hand."

25. As in the New York sketch, this also contains an authentication/dedication in Pepoli's hand, written in London when he was teaching Italian literature at University College:

This sketch of the principal moments in the 2.nd Act of *I Puritani* was the first idea for the layout of Scenes, etc., etc., that I dictated to our dear Bellini, when the illness of my poor eyes made it absolutely impossible for me to write.

This first, shapeless sketch that I imagined and dictated, has the sole but great value of being written in the hand of the gentle Sicilian Maestro, and will serve as a memory to the worthy Princess Linguaglossa of when it was written, and of when it was given to her

in London 1 June 1840.

by her humble servant Carlo Pepoli.

Above this is written another statement, this time by Rocco Pagliara, librarian of the Conservatorio di San Pietro a Majella in Naples at the beginning of this century:

This writing is in Bellini's hand, and the annotation is by Count Pepoli, librettist of *I Puritani*.

Rocco Pagliara.

26. The name of this character changes in the various versions of Paisiello's opera: in the original version, the "Commedia in prosa ed in verso per musica tradotta dal francese" (*opéra-comique* in prose and verse translated from the French) by Marsollier, which was first performed at the court theater of Caserta in 1789, she was Susanna; by the time of the first public peformance at the Teatro dei Fiorentini in Naples in 1790, she had become Elisa; in the performances of the "commedia in prosa e in verso" at the Teatro di San Moisè in Venice in 1792 and 1796, and then in the other Venetian performances up to the revival at the Teatro La Fenice in 1842, the character bears the name of Marianna. In general it is clear that the name of Nina's governess is always Elisa when this attempt at an Italian *opéra-comique* becomes the "dramma giocoso in due atti" that was so successful on the Italian stage, from performances at the court theater of Parma in Carnival 1794, to the revivals at Florence's Teatro della Pergola in spring 1796, at Milan's La Scala in 1804, to the revival at the Teatro Carcano (again in Milan) in the summer of 1829, when the protagonist was sung by Giuditta Pasta.

27. Bellini, *Epistolario*, 431n.2.

28. There would eventually be ten lines, as we see in the libretto for the first performance at La Scala, Milan: "Piangon le ciglia—si spezza il cor / L'inferma figlia—morrà d'amor. / Il duol l'invase. La vidi errante / Tra folte piante... Or per sue case / Gridando va: pietà... pietà!" [With weeping eyes—with breaking heart / The poor, sick daughter—will die of love. / Grief invades her. I saw her wandering / in the dense undergrowth... Now through her apartments / Crying go: mercy... mercy!] (*I Puritani e i Cavalieri.* Opera seria in tre parti da rappresentarsi nell'Imp. Reg. Teatro alla Scala il Carnevale 1835–36, Milano per Luigi di Giacomo Pirola, 1835, 27). Notice the variants with the version that appears in the vocal score.

29. Bellini, *Epistolario*, 431–32.

30. See the letter to Florimo dated 4 October 1834; in ibid., 442.

31. One detail of Cambi's edition (ibid., 429) is clearly in error. Instead of "quartet" it reads "4th act," which is impossible since all versions of Paisiello's opera are in two acts. The "quartet" that Bellini refers to is the musical number that ends the first act of the "dramma giocoso," sung by Nina, il Conte, il Pastore and Elisa: "Come! ohimè! partir

degg'io." This piece became something of a "classic" during the first half of the nineteenth century, Ricordi including it in the *Antologia Classica Musicale Pubblicata dalla Gazzetta Musicale di Milano*, vol. 5 (Milan, 1846), n. 7.

32. Giorgio was written for Luigi Lablache, and he sang the role at the premiere.

33. Bellini, *Epistolario*, 437.

34. Giulia Grisi was the first Elvira, and the role was created with her voice in mind.

35. Bellini, *Epistolario*, 439.

36. Ibid., 486.

37. Ibid., 433.

38. From a letter to Florimo dated 13 October 1834; in ibid., 455.

39. For a detailed description of the differences between the Parisian and Neapolitan versions, and for information on the material belonging to the Naples version, see Friedrich Lippmann, *Vincenzo Bellini und die Italienische Opera seria seiner Zeit* (see chap. 10, n.2), 390–94.

40. From a letter to Florimo dated 30 November 1834; in Bellini, *Epistolario*, 487.

41. From a letter to Florimo dated 4 October 1834; in ibid., 442.